THE HORNBLOWER COMPANION

C. S. Forester was born in 1899 and turned to full time writing after the success of his first novel, *Payment Deferred* (1926). He is, however, best known for his creation of the fictional British naval officer, Horatio Hornblower. The ten completed Hornblower novels recount stirring adventures in the Royal Navy during the era of the Napoleonic wars and paint a vivid picture of the Senior Service at a time when it grew to dominate the world's oceans. He also wrote biography and travel books; he died in 1966.

C. S. FORESTER

The
HORNBLOWER
Companion

With Maps and Drawings by Samuel H. Bryant

NAVAL INSTITUTE PRESS
Annapolis, Maryland

Cover painting
A detail from *'Vanguard* in heavy weather off Toulon' by Geoff Hunt RSMA
An artist signed limited edition of the painting is available from
Richard Lucraft Limited Editions
Telephone +44 (0) 171 935 0818 for a colour brochure

First published by Michael Joseph Ltd, London, in 1964
This edition first published in Great Britain in 1998
by Chatham Publishing, 61 Frith Street, London W1V 5TA

Published and distributed in the United States of America and Canada
by the Naval Institute Press, 118 Maryland Avenue,
Annapolis, Maryland 21402–5035

Library of Congress Catalog Card No. 98-67705

ISBN 1–55750-347–8

This edition authorized for sale only in the United States of America,
its territories and possessions, and Canada.

Manufactured in Great Britain

Contents

The Hornblower Atlas

Map 1 * General Map

PERHAPS it is significant that there was no need to include the Orient in this map; perhaps it is significant that, except for a single foray into the Pacific, Hornblower's activities were confined, during the thirty years 1793 to 1823, to the Atlantic Ocean and its accessory seas, the Baltic, the Mediterranean, and the Caribbean. The destiny of the world was decided in the Atlantic, although it should be remembered that the Royal Navy escorted conquering armies as far as Manila and Java. It may be considered equally significant that Hornblower saw so much service in the Caribbean. The West Indies were of the greatest economic importance throughout this period; the prosperity of London depended to a very great extent on the control of the sugar islands, and that dependence continued until the emancipation of the slaves and the development of the beet sugar industry, and the growth of a hundred new economic factors, relegated the islands to comparative unimportance as Hornblower was entering into his fifties.

This is all very true and very solemn. But perhaps there is another point to be borne in mind, and that is that – by a coincidence – these were the only waters with which Hornblower's biographer was familiar while writing about the closing years of the Napoleonic Wars.

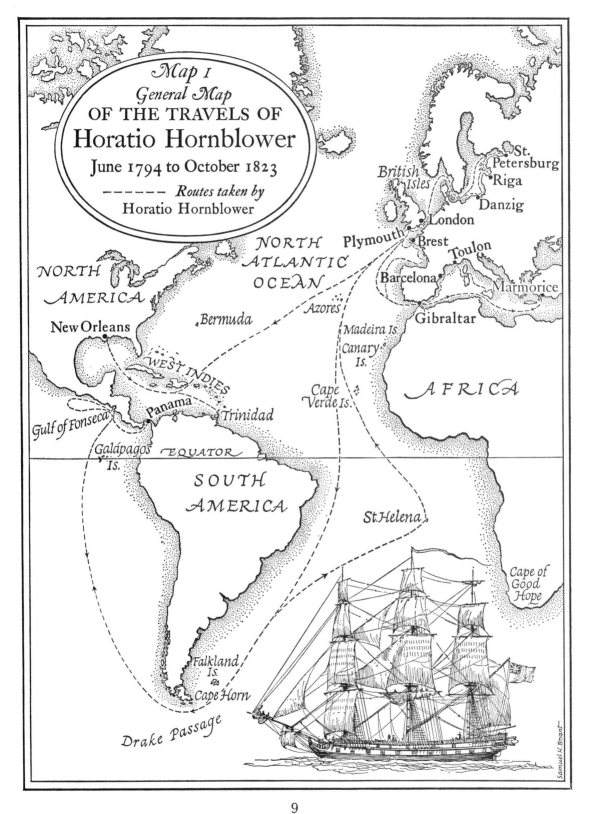

Map I
General Map
OF THE TRAVELS OF
Horatio Hornblower
June 1794 to October 1823

------ Routes taken by
Horatio Hornblower

NORTH
ATLANTIC
OCEAN

NORTH
AMERICA

British
Isles

St.
Petersburg
Riga
Danzig

London
Plymouth
Brest
Toulon
Barcelona
Marmorice
Gibraltar

New Orleans

Bermuda

Azores

Madeira Is.
Canary
Is.

AFRICA

WEST INDIES

Panama
Trinidad

Gulf of Fonseca

Cape
Verde Is.

Galápagos
Is.

EQUATOR

SOUTH
AMERICA

St. Helena

Cape of
Good
Hope

Falkland
Is.
Cape Horn

Drake Passage

Samuel H. Bryant

9

Map 2 * MR. MIDSHIPMAN HORNBLOWER
Chapters 2, 3 and 5 * June, 1794
Bay of Biscay

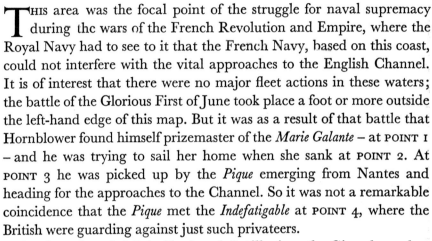

THIS area was the focal point of the struggle for naval supremacy during the wars of the French Revolution and Empire, where the Royal Navy had to see to it that the French Navy, based on this coast, could not interfere with the vital approaches to the English Channel. It is of interest that there were no major fleet actions in these waters; the battle of the Glorious First of June took place a foot or more outside the left-hand edge of this map. But it was as a result of that battle that Hornblower found himself prizemaster of the *Marie Galante* – at POINT 1 – and he was trying to sail her home when she sank at POINT 2. At POINT 3 he was picked up by the *Pique* emerging from Nantes and heading for the approaches to the Channel. So it was not a remarkable coincidence that the *Pique* met the *Indefatigable* at POINT 4, where the British were guarding against just such privateers.

At a later date *Indefatigable* chased *Papillon* into the Gironde, and at a later date still, out in the Bay at POINT 5, well clear of the lee shores during the winter gales, *Indefatigable* met the French frigate trying to break out into the open Atlantic by the southern route.

POINT 1: Capture of the *Marie Galante*. POINT 2: Sinking of the *Marie Galante*. POINT 3: Encounter with the *Pique*. POINT 4: Meeting of *Pique* and *Indefatigable*. POINT 5: Position of battle in chapter 5.

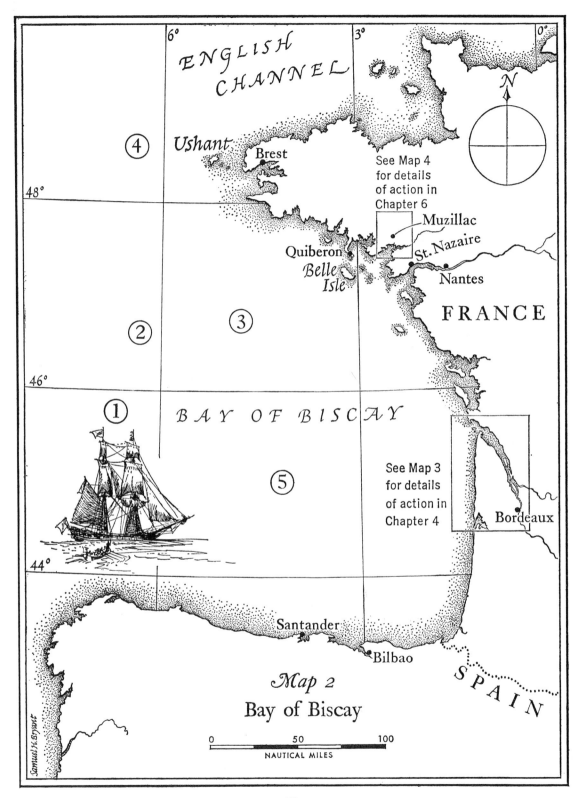

6° 3° 0°

ENGLISH CHANNEL

④ Ushant

Brest

48°

See Map 4
for details
of action in
Chapter 6

Muzillac

Quiberon St. Nazaire

Belle
Isle

Nantes

② ③

FRANCE

46°

BAY OF BISCAY

①

⑤

See Map 3
for details
of action in
Chapter 4

Bordeaux

44°

Santander

Bilbao

S P A I N

Map 2
Bay of Biscay

0 50 100
NAUTICAL MILES

Samuel H. Bryant

Map 3 * MR. MIDSHIPMAN HORNBLOWER
Chapter 4 * September, 1794
The Gironde

A TYPICAL example of the sort of operation carried out scores of times during the French Wars, when French ships crept along the coast from the shelter of one battery to the next, with British ships eagerly seeking an opportunity to attack. In this case complete surprise was achieved; the French crew had spent many nights at anchor here and there, and the standard precautions against night attack had fallen into routine, and there was no reason apparent to them why this night should produce an attack more than any other.

The indispensable factor on the British side was seamanship. There was the skill which brought the *Indefatigable* in over the horizon at night from POINT 1 exactly to her correct anchorage at POINT 3. There was the organization and the equipment which sent the manned boats off without an instant's delay. There was the navigating ability of Lieutenant Eccles in taking the boats up by an unexpected (and unwatched) route over half-tide shoals to attack the *Papillon* at POINT 2. Finally there was the ability to set sail in complete darkness in a completely unknown ship and to bring her down with the tide. Resolution played its part as well; there would only be this one night when the tide was at flood an hour before sunrise. A day of procrastination, a night to think it over, and the opportunity would have passed.

POINT 1: Sunset position of *Indefatigable*. POINT 2: *Papillon* at anchor. POINT 3: Midnight position of *Indefatigable*.

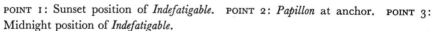

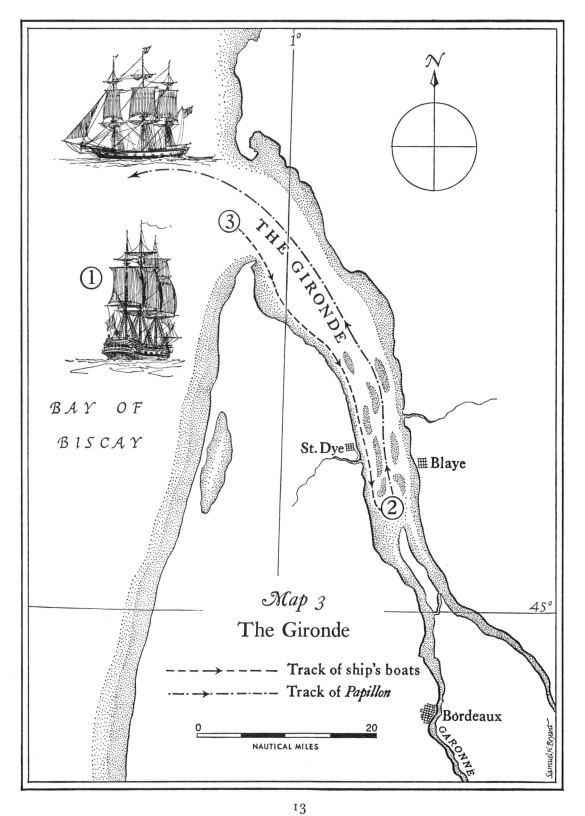

① ②

③

N

THE GIRONDE

BAY OF
BISCAY

1°

St. Dye ⊞

⊞ Blaye

45°

Map 3
The Gironde

– – – → – – – Track of ship's boats
–·– → –·– Track of *Papillon*

0   20
NAUTICAL MILES

⊞ Bordeaux

GARONNE

Samuel H. Bryant

Map 4 * MR. MIDSHIPMAN HORNBLOWER

Chapter 6 * July 20, 1795

The Beach at Muzillac

As a matter of history on this day an actual landing was effected by a Royalist army at Quiberon, a few inches to the left of this map. That landing ended in disaster far worse than this one in which Hornblower took part; it would have been by no means an unnecessary precaution to make an additional landing on the beach at Muzillac to guard the flank of the main force from troops advancing up the main road from Nantes.

Nowadays this coast is dotted with *plages* crowded in the summer with holiday-makers. For them it would only be a brief excursion to visit the beach where Hornblower landed (POINT 2), and to see the bridge which he helped to blow up (POINT 4), and it might even be possible to identify the inn where he slept in the village of Muzillac. But it must be remembered that since 1795 the cutting of new roads, the draining of marshes, and extensive building and rebuilding have changed the landscape considerably.

The disaster that overtook the expedition largely resulted from faulty intelligence work; no one had any knowledge that there was a strong mobile force at Vannes able to come down at POINT 5 on the unguarded flank.

POINT 1: Anchorage of *Sophia* and *Indefatigable*. POINT 2: Landing beach. POINT 3: Ford and position of 43rd. POINT 4: Causeway and bridge. POINT 5: Start of main French attack.

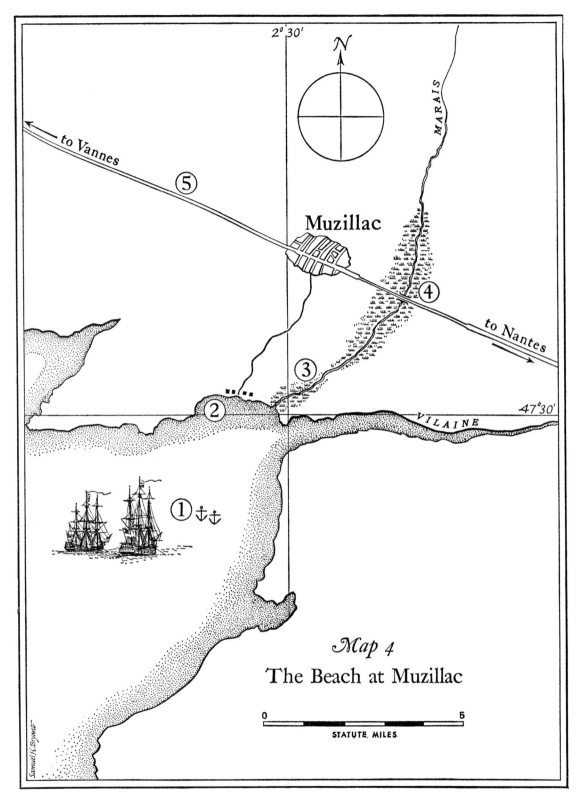

2° 30'

𝒩

to Vannes

⑤

Muzillac

MARAIS

④

to Nantes

③

② ■■■■

47° 30'

VILAINE

① ⚓⚓

Map 4

The Beach at Muzillac

0   5

STATUTE MILES

Samuel H. Bryant

Map 5 * MR. MIDSHIPMAN HORNBLOWER
Chapters 7 and 8 * January, 1796 and March, 1796
Straits of Gibraltar

THE Spanish galleys that Hornblower fought had a real existence; they had been continued in service up to this date largely because of Spanish conservatism – no one had yet taken the necessary steps to decommission them, especially as convicted criminals were easily disposed of by setting them to the oar. As late as 1800, Keith, at the siege of Genoa, captured a Genoese galley. But the galleys were occasionally useful in a calm when their manoeuvrability and the two heavy guns in their bows enabled them to harass temporarily helpless shipping.

It was often difficult to effect a passage of the Straits of Gibraltar in a westerly direction, owing to the constant set of the current inwards, the presence of westerly winds, and the frequent calms – Nelson was sorely handicapped by these conditions in his pursuit of Villeneuve in 1805.

POINT 1: First encounter with the Spanish galleys. POINT 2: Battle with the galleys. POINT 3: Fire ships in the Bay.

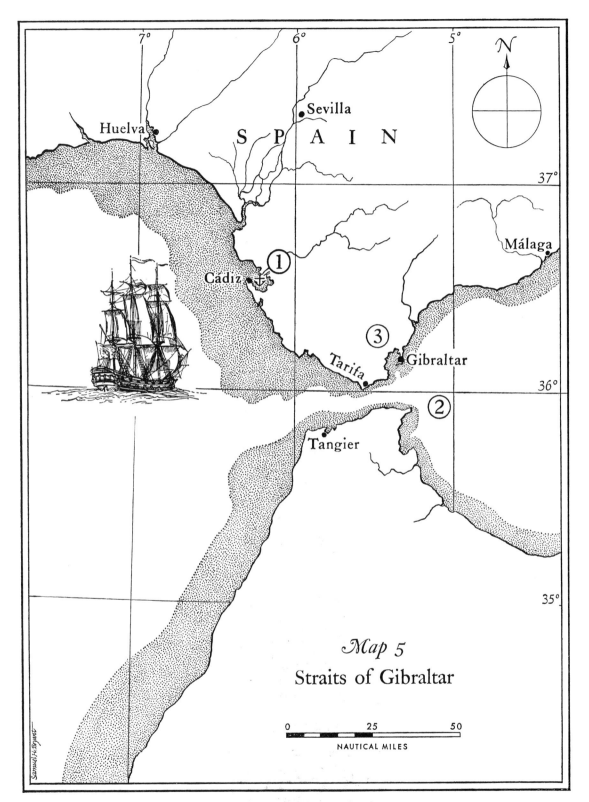

7°   6°   5°

N

● Sevilla

Huelva ●

S   P   A   I   N

37°

Málaga ●

① Cádiz ●

③

Tarifa   Gibraltar ●

36°

②

Tangier ●

35°

Map 5
Straits of Gibraltar

0   25   50

NAUTICAL MILES

Samuel H. Bryant

Map 6 * MR. MIDSHIPMAN HORNBLOWER
Chapter 9 * July, 1796
The Cruise of the *Caroline*

THE Barbary Coast was an important source of fresh meat for the garrison at Gibraltar and for the fleet which watched Toulon and Cádiz, especially when Spain (as at this time) was hostile. Twenty tons of meat a day were needed, without counting waste and offal, which meant that the harassed supply services had to procure over a hundred of the scrubby Berber cattle every single day. Pork, of course, was unobtainable on this Mohammedan coast, and the British sailor – even though in his childhood he had considered himself lucky to eat meat once a week – resented being given mutton. So that from Sallee all the way round to Algiers, British supply ships came in to buy cattle, paying for them in gold or in gunpowder (which was nearly as precious to the Deys and the Beys) while worried consuls strove to keep these capricious monarchs in a neutral frame of mind.

Perhaps it is worthy of remark that while Hornblower was beating about in the *Caroline*, waiting for his quarantine to end, General Bonaparte was conquering Northern Italy in his triumphant first campaign as commander in chief.

POINT 1: Hornblower assumes command of the *Caroline*. POINT 2: First landing for water. POINT 3: Second landing for water and encounter with Spanish *guardacosta*. POINT 4: Cargo delivered.

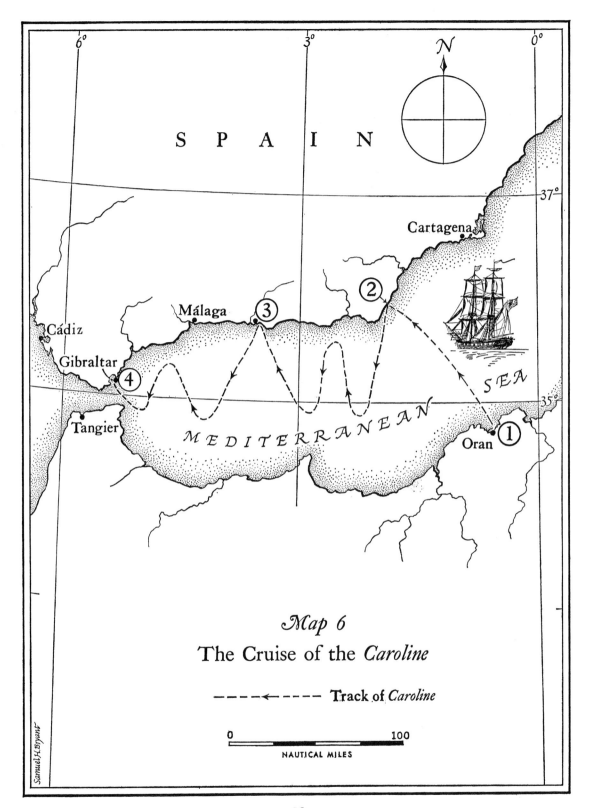

SPAIN

Cartagena

Málaga ③ ②

Cádiz

Gibraltar ④

Tangier

MEDITERRANEAN SEA

Oran ①

Map 6

The Cruise of the *Caroline*

— — — ◄ — — — Track of *Caroline*

0   100

NAUTICAL MILES

Samuel H. Bryant

Map 7 ∗ MR. MIDSHIPMAN HORNBLOWER
Chapter 10 ∗ November, 1797
El Ferrol

THE Spanish ports of El Ferrol and La Coruña, with their excellent harbours, suffered in an exaggerated degree from the disability that plagued Brest; they were so far from the centre of things, and their overland communications were so unsatisfactory, that when they were deprived by blockade of their sea communications they languished and were unable to function satisfactorily as naval bases. This may explain why a Spanish merchant ship was trying to run the blockade in a November gale; she could carry in her holds as much as five hundred ox wagons could bring over the mountains. It was unlucky for her, and extremely lucky for Hornblower, that she split her main-topsail at the crucial moment.

Hornblower, of course, made instant use of the opportunity presented to him, smoothing not only his path to freedom, but also the path of the novelist who undertook his biography.

POINT 1: Hornblower's lookout post. POINT 2: Spanish ship loses main-topsail. POINT 3: Wreck. POINT 4: Track along which fishing boat was dragged. POINT 5: Fishing boat launching site.

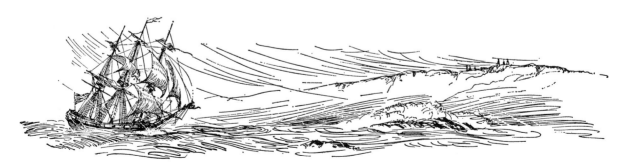

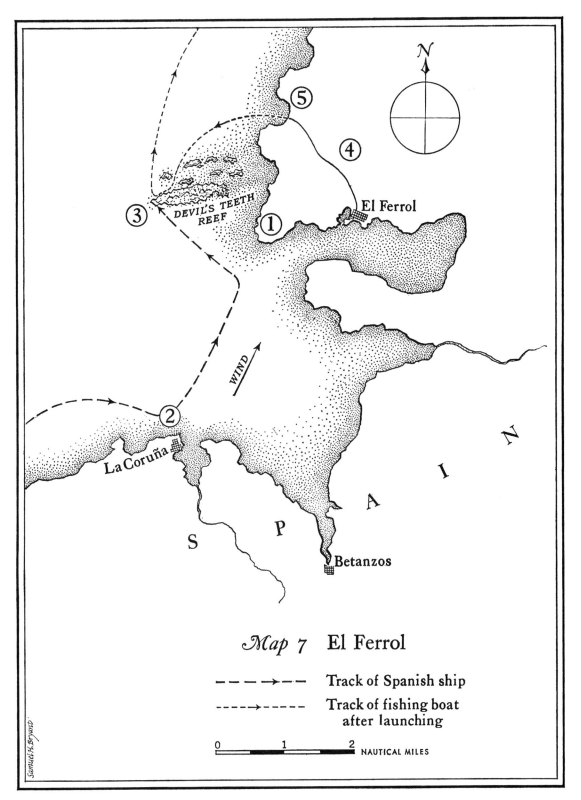

N

⑤

④

③

DEVIL'S TEETH
REEF

①

El Ferrol

WIND

②

La Coruña

S   P   A   I   N

Betanzos

Map 7   El Ferrol

— — →— — —   Track of Spanish ship

- - - →- - - -   Track of fishing boat
after launching

0   1   2   NAUTICAL MILES

Map 8 * LIEUTENANT HORNBLOWER
Chapters 7 to 17 * June to August, 1800
Santo Domingo

HERE came H.M.S. *Renown*, running on a southwesterly course before the northeast trades, with an insane captain confined below and an exacting mission ahead of her. When Hornblower's biographer steamed through the Mona Passage on an opposite course in the *Margaret Johnson* much more than a century later he was still comfortably unaware that the twin silhouettes of Mona and Monita had any special significance for him, nor that Samaná Bay on his left hand had been the scene of such desperate action. He was, in fact, not only ignorant of the theory of handling red-hot shot, but he was still some days from hearing (from his inner self) even the name of Horatio Hornblower. Yet for some reason he carried home with him the clearest memory of Cape Engaño and of the rolling hills of Santo Domingo. POINT 2 is of minor importance, referring to the arrival of the news of the Peace of Amiens, which meant that Hornblower's first and temporary promotion to commander would be disallowed by the Admiralty.

POINT 1: Beginning of chapter 7. POINT 2: Encounter between *Renown* and *Clara*.

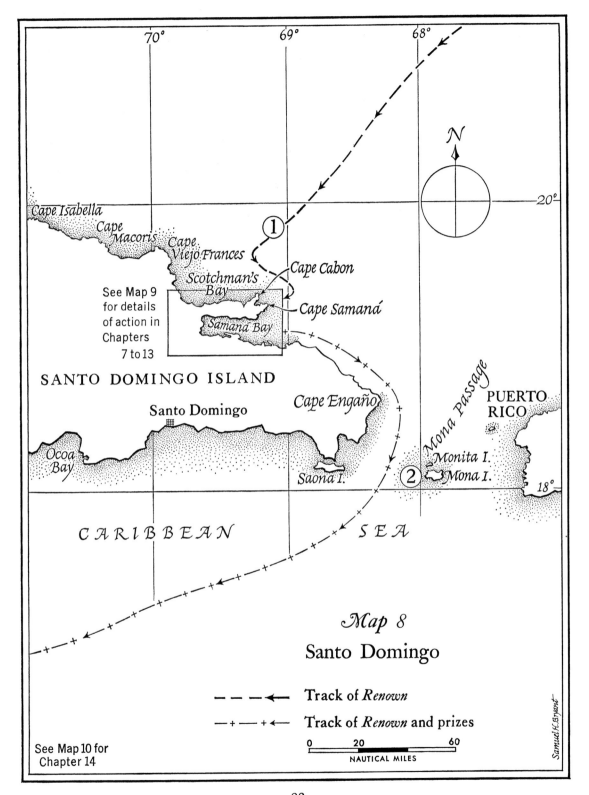

70°　　　　　　　69°　　　　　　　68°

N

Cape Isabella

Cape Macoris

Cape Viejo *Cape Frances*

① 20°

Cape Cabon

Scotchman's Bay

See Map 9
for details
of action in
Chapters
7 to 13

Cape Samaná

Samana Bay

SANTO DOMINGO ISLAND

Santo Domingo

Cape Engaño

Mona Passage

PUERTO
RICO

Ocoa Bay

Monita I.

Mona I.

Saona I.

②

18°

C A R I B B E A N   S E A

Map 8

Santo Domingo

Track of *Renown*

Track of *Renown* and prizes

See Map 10 for
Chapter 14

0　　　　20　　　　　　60

NAUTICAL MILES

Samuel H. Bryant

Map 9 * LIEUTENANT HORNBLOWER
Chapters 7 to 13 * July, 1800
The Gulf of Samaná

IT WAS quite inevitable that, to make its power fully felt, the Royal Navy should have entered upon amphibious actions. The naval history of the twenty years after 1794 is studded with them, and, naturally, they were nearly all undertaken at points where the enemy's strength on land interfered with the full exertion of sea power. There are scores of examples of an extemporized landing force storming a battery which was giving protection to hostile shipping. The defending powers, with an infinite number of points to garrison, necessarily left many points weak, and a mobile seaborne force could often find a landing place, so that, handled resolutely and rapidly, it could attack the shore defences unexpectedly from the rear. The configuration of the land at the east end of Santo Domingo offered a golden opportunity for such a stroke; it was possible to land a force at nightfall on the north shore at POINT 2 and to move across the neck to storm at dawn the fort which denied entrance to the bay. The existence of another battery at the southern side of the entrance – now alerted to its danger and therefore not so easily stormed – made it necessary to drag the nine-pounder to POINT 7 and make the anchorage of the merchant shipping uncomfortable enough to compel them to come out.

POINT 1: *Renown* runs aground. POINT 2: Landing place for attack on Fort. POINT 3: Track of landing party in attack on Fort. POINT 4: Anchorage of Spanish merchant ships. POINT 5: Spanish merchant ships hit by red-hot shot. POINT 6: Landing spot of nine-pounder. POINT 7: Firing position of nine-pounder.

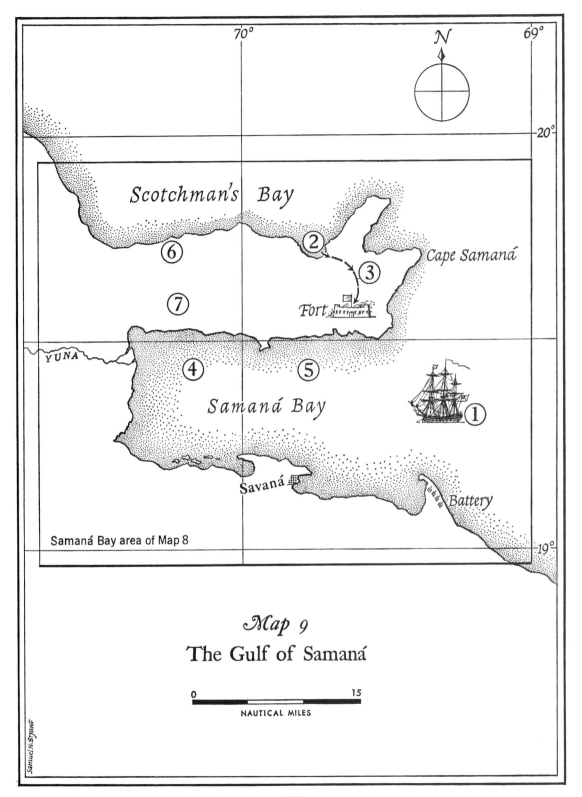

70°

69°

N

20°

Scotchman's Bay

⑥

②

③

Cape Samaná

⑦

Fort

YUNA

④

⑤

Samaná Bay

①

Savaná

Battery

Samaná Bay area of Map 8

19°

Map 9
The Gulf of Samaná

0   15

NAUTICAL MILES

Samuel H. Bryant

Map 10 ∗ LIEUTENANT HORNBLOWER
Chapter 14 ∗ July, 1800
The Caribbean

IT WAS during the long run from the Mona Passage to Jamaica that the Spanish prisoners rose on their captors and momentarily secured possession of H.M.S. *Renown*. Thanks to Hornblower the ship was quickly recaptured; it was a phenomenon frequently observed in sailing ship days (the capture of the *Papillon* is an example) that once a party has secured possession of the main deck, with control of the management of the ship, it was possible to retain that control although a larger, hostile force was down below. Battened down, so that even if they could force the hatches they could only emerge one by one, the dispossessed crew was comparatively helpless – they could set the ship on fire or blow up the magazine, but these were suicidal expedients, although both were known to occur. It is strange that (as far as the present writer's reading goes) it never occurred to anyone to adopt the simple expedient of sawing through the tiller ropes.

It was a slight misfortune for Hornblower that at this point in his history his biographer was more interested in the deeds of Lieutenant Bush, so that Hornblower's clear thinking in uniting the prize crews from all the prizes before launching his counter-attack from the *Gaditana* (later named *Retribution*, aptly enough) has not received all the recognition it deserves. Despite this omission on the part of his biographer, Hornblower at least received from Admiral Lambert the abortive appointment to the command of the *Retribution*.

POINT 1: Prisoners take over *Renown* and Hornblower recaptures her.

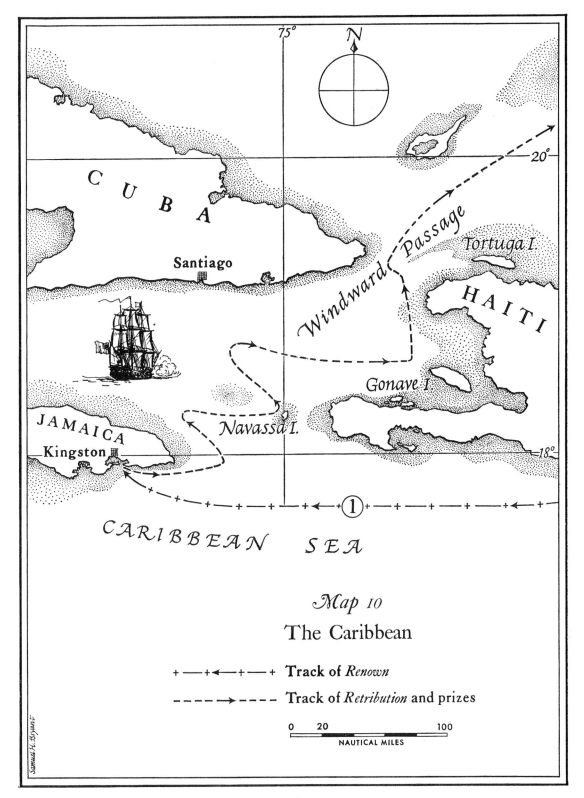

75°

N

CUBA

Santiago

20°

Windward Passage

Tortuga I.

HAITI

Gonave I.

JAMAICA

Kingston

Navassa I.

①

18°

CARIBBEAN SEA

Samuel H. Bryant

Map 10

The Caribbean

+ — + ← + — + **Track of** *Renown*

- - - → - - - **Track of** *Retribution* **and prizes**

0   20   100

NAUTICAL MILES

Map II * HORNBLOWER AND THE *HOTSPUR*

Chapters 4 to 25 * April, 1803 to July, 1805

Approaches to Brest

THIS map is studded with reference points, the result of the fact that Hornblower spent two years in the blockade of Brest, so that a good deal of action could be expected there. Quite a number of men, less fortunate than Hornblower, spent ten whole years consecutively on this blockade duty, experiencing, in those hard conditions, the transition from youth to middle age, so that at the end of the war they were quite unfitted for life on land and unable to find employment at sea.

Yachtsmen who are familiar with this coast must always be astonished at the small losses experienced by the large force which watched Brest almost continuously, winter and summer. Only one ship of the line was lost in all those years, and she ran on an uncharted rock. It is remarkable proof of the seamanship of the Royal Navy at this time.

POINT 1: 6 degrees W. longitude: opening of sealed orders. POINT 2: Sighting of the *Deux Frères.* POINT 3: *Hotspur*'s usual patrol route. POINT 4: Peacetime encounter with the *Loire.* POINTS 5 AND 6: Positions of *Hotspur* and *Loire* respectively at wartime encounter. POINT 7. Disablement of the *Loire.* POINT 8: Encounter with French coasters. POINT 9: Dinner on board the *Tonnant.* POINT 10: Landing jetty for shore expedition. POINT 11: Location of signal station. POINT 12: Location of battery. POINT 13: Encampment of French troops. POINT 14: First meeting with French transports. POINT 15: First transport grounded here. POINT 16: Two transports grounded here (on Les Fillettes). POINT 17: Encounter with fourth transport and French frigate. POINT 18: *Grasshopper* dismasted. POINT 19: Mobile battery. POINT 20: *Hibernia*'s usual station.

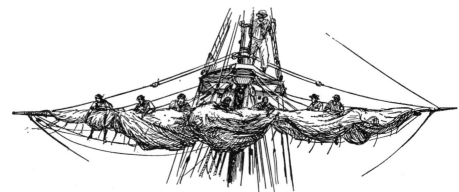

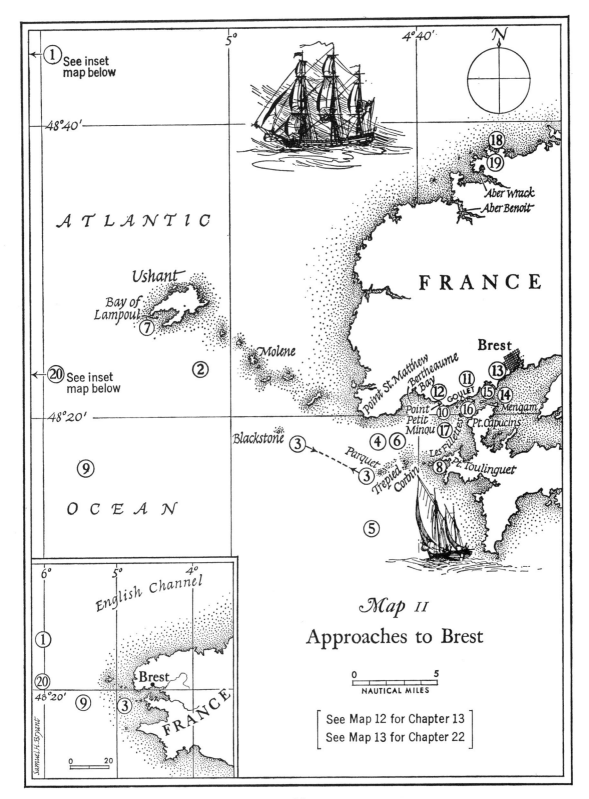

ATLANTIC

48°40'

N

18
19
Aber Wrack
Aber Benoit

FRANCE

Ushant
Bay of Lampoul
7

Molene

Brest
13
11
Point St. Matthew
Bertheaume Bay
12
GOULET
15
14
10
16
Mengam
Point Petit Minou
17
Pt. Capucins

2

20 See inset map below

48°20'

Blackstone
3
Parquet
Trepied
Corbin
4 6
Les Fillettes
Pt. Toulinguet
8
9

OCEAN

3

5

Map II

Approaches to Brest

0   5
NAUTICAL MILES

[See Map 12 for Chapter 13]
[See Map 13 for Chapter 22]

1 See inset map below

6°   5°   4°
English Channel
1
20
Brest
48°20'
9
3
FRANCE
0   20

Samuel H. Bryant

Map 12 ∗ HORNBLOWER AND THE *HOTSPUR*

Chapter 13 ∗ October, 1803

Hotspur's Track to Tor Bay

THERE was always the danger with the prevailing westerly winds of being blown up-channel; it was a possibility that had constantly to be borne in mind, and one that influenced strategic thought at least since the days of the Armada. French admirals both during the War of American Independence and the later French Wars were extremely chary of committing themselves beyond a point of no return, even though urged on by Vergennes or Bonaparte. The British Navy had of course the advantage of having good and extensive harbours open to them, but if, during a westerly gale, a ship was forced up-channel beyond the Start she was likely to find difficulty in regaining her station as a result of having to beat out in the narrower waters to the eastward. Hence the importance of Tor Bay as an anchorage – Plymouth was difficult of egress until the breakwaters were built, while Falmouth suffered from poor inland communication. Ever since the loss of Sir Cloudesley Shovel on the Scillies the British had made a study of the tidal sets in the mouth of the Channel, but this need not detract from Hornblower's achievement in making his landfall at Bolt Head.

POINT 1: Encounter with *Naiad*. POINT 2: Course altered to put wind on port quarter. POINT 3: Sounding taken here.

E N G L A N D

Plymouth

Tor Bay

The Start

Bolt
Head

③

Lizard Pt.

E N G L I S H   C H A N N E L

Guernsey

②

F R A N C E

①Ushant

Brest

Map 12

Hotspur's Track to Tor Bay

→ – – – – → Track of *Hotspur*

0   25   50

NAUTICAL MILES

Samuel H. Bryant

Map 13 * HORNBLOWER AND THE *HOTSPUR*

Chapter 22 * September, 1804

Patrol Area of Moore's Squadron off Cape St Vincent

THERE really was a Captain Graham Moore, who actually was sent to intercept the Spanish treasure fleet at this time, and who patrolled in exactly this fashion. The whole incident of the capture of the *flota* and the subsequent denial of prize money to the captors by the British Government really happened – on the previous occasion, some years earlier, when the *flota* was intercepted, the captors shared millions. Unfortunately the conscientious student who reads the official reports will find no mention either of the *Hotspur* or of the *Félicité* and may naturally experience doubts as to whether there ever was a Captain Hornblower, but if he once accepts Hornblower's existence he may at least agree that Hornblower's action in this case displayed remarkable self-denial as well as the clarity of vision worthy of a hero of fiction.

POINT 1: Patrol area of Moore's squadron. POINT 2: *Hotspur* sights *Félicité*. POINT 3: *Hotspur* disabled.

41°

8°

40°

Lisbon

39°

SPAIN

PORTUGAL

N

7°

6°

Huelva

Cape
St.Vincent

38°

③

②

Málaga

36°30'

①

Cádiz

36°

Gibraltar

Straits of Gibraltar

AFRICA

Map 13

Patrol Area of Moore's Squadron
off Cape St. Vincent

0   25   50

NAUTICAL MILES

Samuel H.Bryant

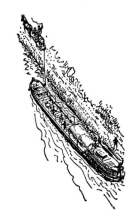

Map 14 * HORNBLOWER AND THE *ATROPOS*

Chapters 1 to 3 * October, 1805

Gloucester to Deptford

BY A fortunate coincidence, Hornblower's biographer happened to have had extensive experience on the rivers and canals of England as well as in other countries. Long before such travel once more became fashionable he captained a boat from London to Llangollen and back again; as a passenger on board there was his elder son, a few months old, who spent three happy months in the tranquillity of the canal waterways disturbed only slightly by the nightmare passages of such tunnels as Blisworth and Braunston. Indeed, the greatest peril to the halcyon peace of those voyages was the fact that the captain happened to be a novelist, engaged at that very time in writing a novel, which was not the easiest thing to do in a small boat of whose crew of three one third was less than six months old. But the experience at least gave him some qualification for writing about Hornblower's journey by canal and river across England with his small son in company.

POINT 1: Sapperton Tunnel. POINT 2: Transfer from canal to river. POINT 3: Supper at Oxford. POINT 4: Transfer to wherry. POINT 5: *Atropos* at anchor (at Deptford).

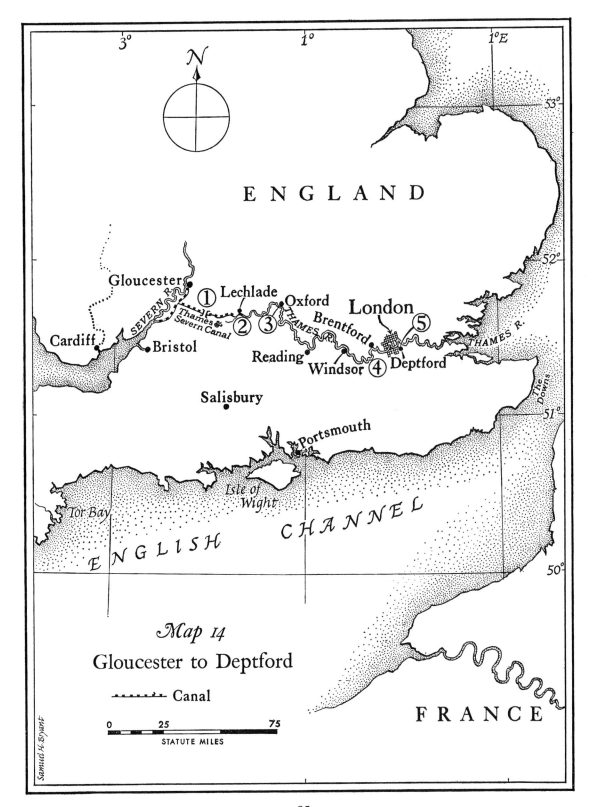

N

ENGLAND

Gloucester

Lechlade ①

Oxford

London

Brentford ⑤

SEVERN

Thames & Severn Canal

② ③ THAMES R.

Cardiff

Bristol

Reading

Windsor ④ Deptford

Salisbury

Portsmouth

Isle of Wight

THAMES R.

The Downs

Tor Bay

ENGLISH CHANNEL

FRANCE

Map 14

Gloucester to Deptford

········ Canal

0   25   75

STATUTE MILES

Samuel H. Bryant

3°   1°   1°E

53°

52°

51°

50°

Map 15 * HORNBLOWER AND THE *ATROPOS*
Chapter 4 * January, 1806
The Thames, Deptford to Westminster

ON another occasion Hornblower's biographer brought his small boat as deck cargo from the Eastern Baltic in a ship which anchored not very far from where *Atropos* anchored in 1806. It made no difference that a violent westerly gale was blowing with deluges of rain while every tug and barge on the river seemed to be moving about at top speed. Over the side the boat had to go, preliminary to the ship going into dock, and down a Jacob's ladder went the biographer and his wife, to steer that boat up-river where racing tugs kicked up washes that appeared to be – and possibly even were – eight feet high and vertical. Only by holding on both with hands and feet were they able to avoid being thrown out bodily as the boat pitched and leaped over the towering waves; even after the passage of London Bridge and the resultant diminution of traffic there was only a small moderation in those waves with the wind against the tide. The terrace of the Houses of Parliament at last afforded a welcome lee where the boat could be bailed out – years later while eating strawberries and cream there on a glorious summer day the writer could afford to smile at the memory. The voyage ended in minor disaster at Vauxhall, just above, with a chastened writer resolved – at least momentarily – to do his adventuring in the future only by the proxy of Hornblower, which might explain the difficulties Hornblower encountered with Nelson's funeral procession.

POINT 1: *Atropos*'s anchorage. POINT 2: Procession forms here: plank started in funeral barge. POINT 3: Bailing commenced. POINT 4: Coffin landed here. POINT 5: Jetty for emergency repairs to funeral barge.

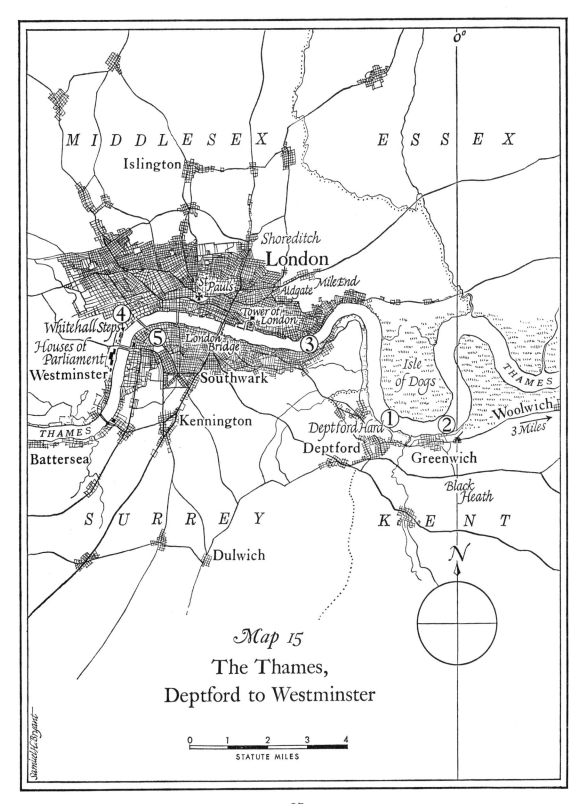

Map 15

The Thames,
Deptford to Westminster

0   1   2   3   4
STATUTE MILES

37

Map 16 * HORNBLOWER AND THE ATROPOS

Chapter 8 * May, 1806

The Downs

CHILDHOOD memory led to the capture of the *Vengeance* by the *Atropos* and the recapture of the *Amelia Jane*. A little boy was playing some game with a foreign visitor, a game involving writing down the score, and he puzzled over the curious crossbars which the visitor put on his 7's. The visitor was a grown man and should know better; it was an affront to the little boy's sense of what was proper – he had been taught to write his 7's without crossbars, and children tend to be formalists in matters of petty detail. Later on when the child had grown into a novelist (if that can be called growth) the memory expanded into a story. As it happened, the novelist was preoccupied at that time with naval history, and so the barred 7 appeared on an oar and the *Vengeance* was captured; if the development had occurred during some other phase of the novelist's activities the barred 7 might have appeared in a story of international banking and Hornblower might have been deprived of an adventure.

POINT 1: *Atropos*'s anchorage. POINT 2: *Amelia Jane*'s anchorage. POINT 3: *Vengeance*'s anchorage. POINT 4: Other unidentified ships at anchor.

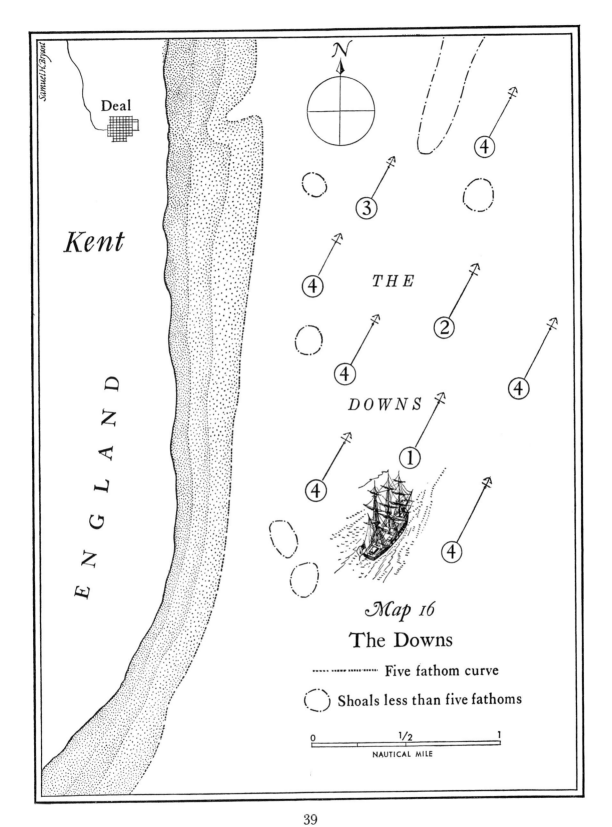

Samuel H. Bryant

Deal

Kent

E N G L A N D

N

THE

DOWNS

Map 16

The Downs

- - - - - - - - - Five fathom curve

Shoals less than five fathoms

0   1/2   1

NAUTICAL MILE

39

Map 17 * HORNBLOWER AND THE *ATROPOS*

Chapters 9 to 21 * July, 1806 to January, 1808

The Mediterranean

THE vicissitudes of naval life have been notorious through the ages, but Hornblower in his career was the victim of the whims of a more capricious destiny even than usual. It was fitting, perhaps, that a few casual words dropped by an admiral should have sent him all the way up the Mediterranean to the Turkish coast. The admiral was one of the most distinguished in the distinguished list of British admirals, and he not only reminded Hornblower's biographer of the potential interest of Marmorice Bay as a location for the activities of Hornblower's pearl divers, but he also presented him with a copy of the *Mediterranean Pilot*, volume 5, containing (among much else) the sailing directions for the area – soundings and bearings in 1950 were hardly different from those in 1806. So to Marmorice Bay went Hornblower and his pearl divers; later he encountered the Spanish frigate *Castilla* so that years later while negotiating with El Supremo he could wear the gold-hilted sword presented to him in commemoration of that event.

POINT 1: McCullum comes on board. POINT 2: First rendezvous point. POINT 3: Rendezvous with Mediterranean fleet. POINT 4: McCullum wounded in duel. POINT 5: Becalmed here for a day. POINT 6: Operation on McCullum. POINT 7: Next rendezvous with Collingwood. POINT 8: Treasure discharged. POINT 9: *Castilla* pursues. POINT 10: Mr Prince falls overboard. POINT 11: Action with *Castilla*. POINT 12: *Atropos* purchased by King of Sicily.

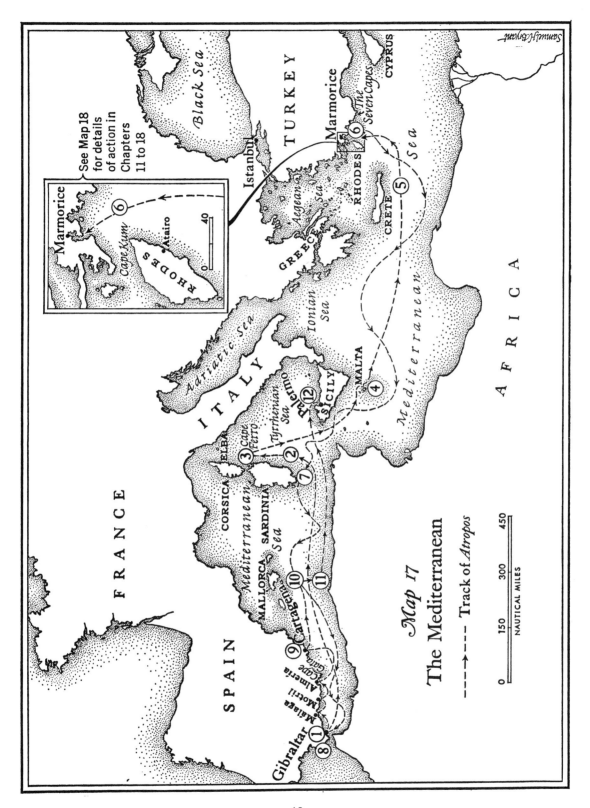

See Map 18
for details
of action in
Chapters
11 to 18

Map 17
The Mediterranean
– – – – Track of *Atropos*

0   150   300   450
NAUTICAL MILES

Samuel H. Bryant

41

Map 18 * HORNBLOWER AND THE ATROPOS

Chapters 11 to 18 * March, 1807

Marmorice Bay

IT WAS as a result of the admiral's gift that Hornblower was able to make such a successful escape from Marmorice Bay under the guns of the *Mejidieh*. Hornblower owed a good deal, too, to the fortunate chance that the wind was northeasterly on that particular night, but the lucky man is always the one who is ready to take advantage of good fortune, and who has a biographer willing to load the dice in his favour. Leaving fantasy aside, it is worth noting that Marmorice Bay had actually been the anchorage of the fleet and convoy when Keith was assembling his forces for the reconquest of Egypt in 1801, and a good deal of curious information can be gleaned from the Keith Papers written at that period. Fact can frequently rival fiction.

POINT 1: *Atropos*'s anchorage. POINT 2: Position of wreck. POINT 3: *Mejidieh*'s anchorage.

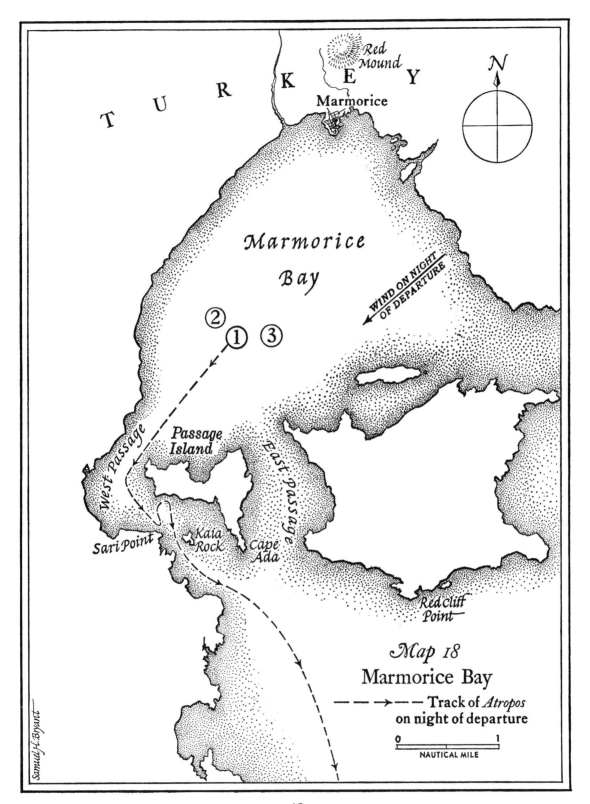

TURKEY

Red
Mound

Marmorice

𝒩

Marmorice
Bay

WIND ON NIGHT
OF DEPARTURE

② ① ③

West Passage

Passage
Island

East Passage

Sari Point

Kaia
Rock

Cape
Ada

Red Cliff
Point

Map 18
Marmorice Bay

– – – – ➤ – – – Track of *Atropos*
on night of departure

0   1
NAUTICAL MILE

Samuel H. Bryant

43

Map 19 * THE HAPPY RETURN or BEAT TO QUARTERS

Chapters 1 to 21 * June to August, 1808

Pacific Coast of Central America

THE wind still blows in the Gulf of Tehuantepec, just as it blew in Hornblower's time; here the trade winds, balked elsewhere by the great mass of America, come funnelling over the comparatively low and narrow Isthmus, descending to the sea as a warm gale which on occasions – as during *Lydia's* fight with *Natividad* – will suddenly die out, like the turning off of a tap, on account of some unknown meteorological disturbance to the northeast. Farther along the coast, approaching Panama, the wind is variable and fluky; Hornblower, as he plied up and down along it with the ebb and flow of war, must have had a certain amount of good fortune in finding fair winds. But by this time he had spent, even making due allowance for leave and time in port, some twelve years actually at sea, and during that time a man of his studious and inquiring disposition had inevitably acquired a flair for wind prediction as well as the skill to make the best use of every favouring slant.

POINT 1: First landfall. POINT 2: Encounter with Spanish lugger. POINT 3: Lady Barbara embarks here. POINT 4: Area of final battles between *Lydia* and *Natividad*. POINT 5: Second encounter with Spanish lugger. POINT 6: *Lydia* careened here. POINT 7: Final encounter with Spanish lugger.

Lydia

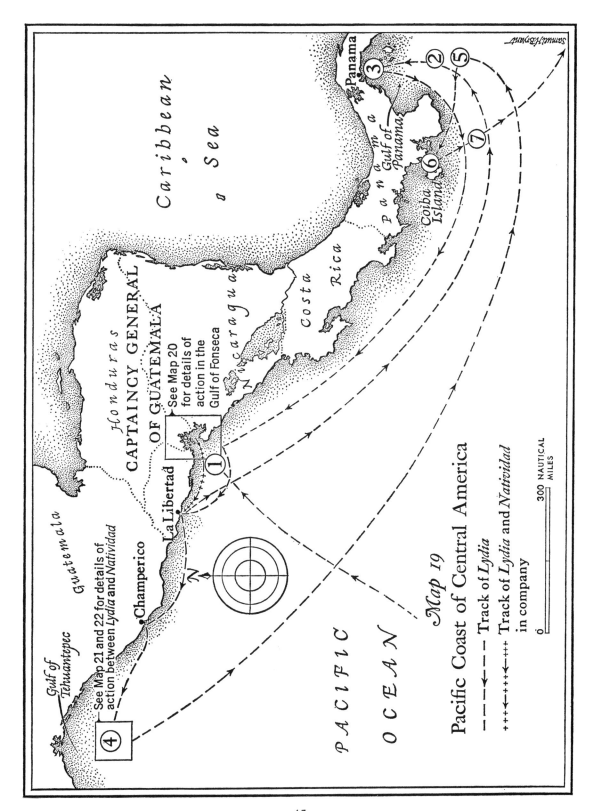

Caribbean

Sea

Honduras

CAPTAINCY GENERAL
OF GUATEMALA

See Map 20
for details of
action in the
Gulf of Fonseca

Guatemala

*Gulf of
Tehuantepec*

See Maps 21 and 22 for details of
action between *Lydia* and *Natividad*

Champerico

La Libertad

①

④

Nicaragua

*Costa
Rica*

Panama

*Gulf of
Panama*

Coiba
Island

Panama

③

②

⑤

⑦

⑥

PACIFIC

OCEAN

Map 19

Pacific Coast of Central America

— — — Track of *Lydia*
++++←++++ Track of *Lydia* and *Natividad*
         in company

0   300 NAUTICAL
                         MILES

SamuelH.Bryant

45

Map 20 * THE HAPPY RETURN *or* BEAT TO QUARTERS
Chapters 1 to 8 * June, 1808
Gulf of Fonseca

NOWADAYS three countries stretch to the sea in the Gulf of Fonseca, so that there are the inevitable customs houses to be found along its shores, but they are just the kind of customs houses one would expect in this area. A brief railway finds a speedy terminus near where El Supremo's house stood – which possibly explains why the explorer will search for it in vain – and yet despite these innovations the Gulf of Fonseca has hardly changed since the *Lydia* anchored there. It is still a place easier – and even quicker – to reach by sea than by air. There are the same lashing rainstorms, the same miserable villages, and the volcanoes still glow at night as when Hornblower first observed them. His biographer was fortunate in having the opportunity to prowl about these mosquito-ridden shores in the *Margaret Johnson*'s motor lifeboat, so that he could see with his own eyes where the *Lydia* laid her ambush behind Meanguera Island, even though he was unaware at the time that such a ship as the *Lydia* had ever existed.

POINT 1: First anchorage of *Lydia*. POINT 2: El Supremo's house. POINT 3: Watering place. POINT 4: Second anchorage of *Lydia*. POINT 5: Capture of *Natividad*.

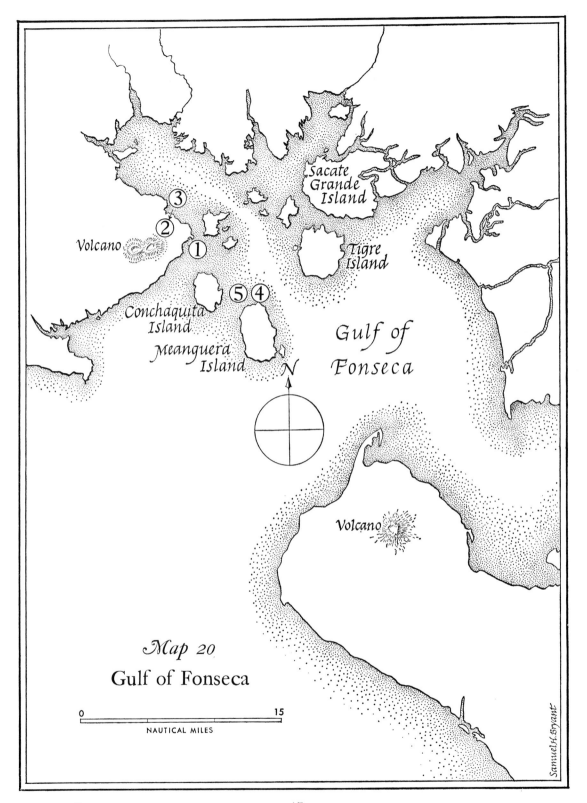

Sacate
Grande
Island

Volcano

Tigre
Island

③

②

①

⑤④

Conchaquita
Island

Meanguera
Island

*Gulf of
Fonseca*

N

Volcano

Map 20
Gulf of Fonseca

0   15

NAUTICAL MILES

Samuel H. Bryant

Map 21 * THE HAPPY RETURN or BEAT TO QUARTERS
Chapters 13 and 14 * July 20, 1808

First Engagement Between *Lydia* and *Natividad*

HERE was a typical single-ship action fought in a brisk wind with unlimited sea room so as to give every advantage to the better-handled ship; it bears a close resemblance to the frigate actions fought in the early part of the War of 1812. The object of the manoeuvres was always the same – to cross the enemy's bow or stern so as to bring to bear the broadside guns opposed only by the very few with which the enemy could reply. Napoleon himself said that war is simple enough; it is only the execution that is difficult. Hornblower had the handier ship, the better-trained crew, and his own quickness of thought, and so he was enabled almost literally to sail rings round his heavier opponent. It was only the damage to her masts and rigging which prevented *Lydia* from winning the battle in this first encounter.

POINT 1: Position of *Lydia* at the time of sighting *Natividad*. POINT 2: Position of *Natividad* at the time of sighting *Lydia*. POINT 3: *Natividad* opens fire with starboard battery. POINT 4: *Lydia* opens fire with starboard battery. POINT 5: *Lydia* rakes *Natividad*'s stern with port battery. POINT 6: *Natividad* alongside *Lydia*; *Lydia* backs main-topsail. POINT 7: *Lydia* rakes *Natividad*'s stern with starboard battery. POINT 8: *Lydia* rakes *Natividad*'s stern with port battery. POINT 9: *Lydia* loses mizzenmast. POINT 10: *Natividad* rakes *Lydia*'s stern. POINT 11: Both ships firing broadsides. POINT 12: *Natividad* loses foremast, ships drift apart.

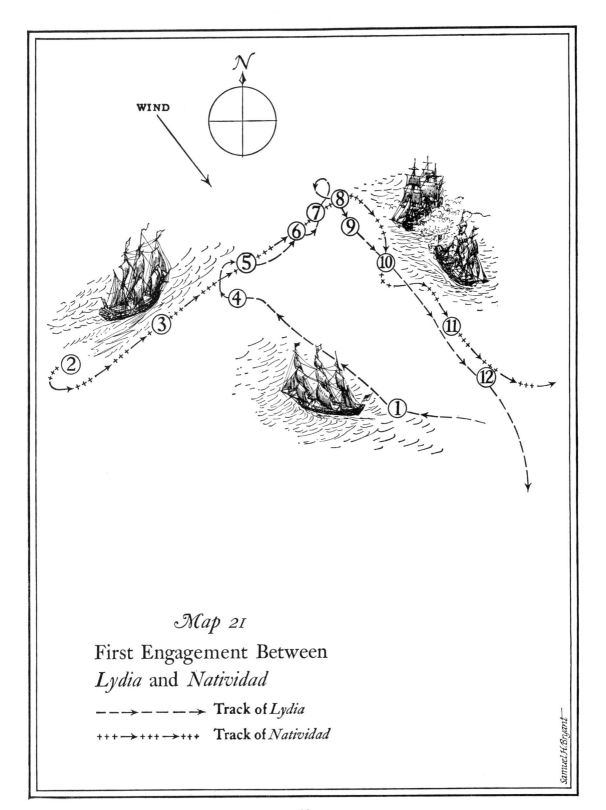

WIND

N

Map 21

First Engagement Between
Lydia and *Natividad*

‐ ‐ ‐→‐ ‐ ‐→ Track of *Lydia*
+++→+++→+++ Track of *Natividad*

Samuel H. Bryant

Map 22 * THE HAPPY RETURN *or* BEAT TO QUARTERS

Chapters 15 to 17 * July 21, 1808

Second Engagement Between *Lydia* and *Natividad*

THE dying away of the wind on the second day of the battle lessened *Lydia*'s advantages so that to a great extent the two ships had to fight it out like unskilled boxers toe to toe. However, *Natividad* had suffered much greater damage on the previous day, and had been less prompt in repairing it, so that *Lydia* was now the more effective ship, and as soon as the wind made itself felt again she was able to rake her helpless opponent. By the traditions of sea warfare at this time *Natividad* should now have surrendered, for she could do her enemy no further harm and her crew were giving their lives for nothing in exchange. In this case the battle was brought to an end by the sinking of the *Natividad*; there were occasional examples during the Napoleonic Wars of wooden ships sinking as the result of gunfire. It is likely that the clumsy two-decker lost so much stability that she rolled her gunports under.

POINT 1: Position of *Lydia* at the time of sighting *Natividad*. POINT 2: Position of *Natividad* at the time of sighting *Lydia*. POINT 3: Wind dies down; *Lydia* starts towing with boats. POINT 4: Wind dies down; *Natividad* starts towing with boats. POINT 5: *Natividad* opens fire with stern chaser. POINT 6: *Lydia*'s launch sunk. POINT 7: *Lydia* opens fire with port battery. POINT 8: *Natividad* loses jury foremast and mainmast. POINT 9: Ships side by side. POINT 10: *Natividad* catches fire and sinks.

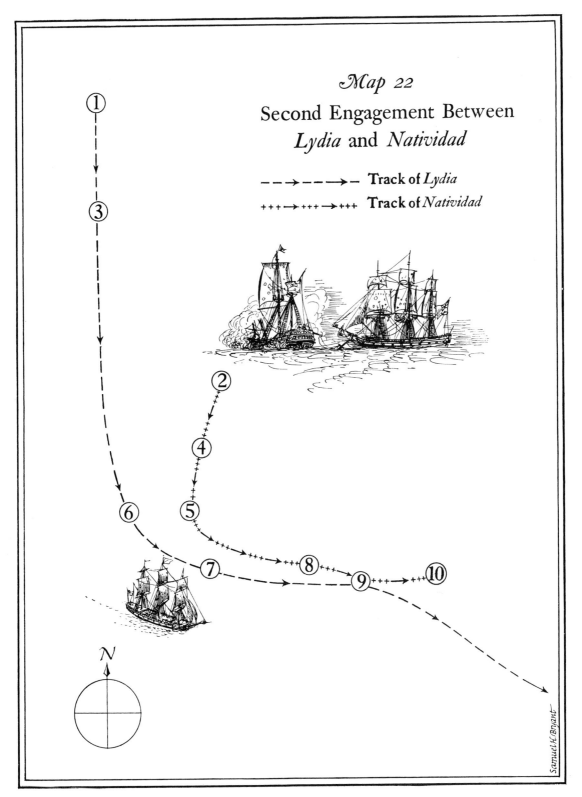

Map 22

Second Engagement Between
Lydia and _Natividad_

– – →– – → **Track of** _Lydia_

+++→+++→+++ **Track of** _Natividad_

N

Samuel H. Bryant

Map 23 * SHIP OF THE LINE and FLYING COLOURS

May, 1810 to June, 1811

General Map of Hornblower's Operations

SOMEWHERE in this book the influence of the Spanish Civil War on the writing of *Ship of the Line* has been mentioned. During those disturbed years there were other factors. The Peninsular and Oriental Steamship Company quoted special fares for the run from London to Marseille and return, because, with most passengers travelling overland to and from Marseille, the ships were nearly empty, and anyone who was not afraid of storms in the Bay could have fourteen days at sea at about the cost of staying in a Pimlico boarding house and in more comfort. The Spanish War was still going on, and Europe was in a turmoil, when Hornblower's biographer made the trip in Hornblower's tracks, writing a thousand words each morning in the quiet of a ship on which he was almost the only passenger. Mussolini's submarines (does anyone remember now?) were misbehaving in the Mediterranean, rather carelessly torpedoing ships suspected of bringing aid to the Republican government, and Hornblower's biographer, coming out on deck at the first light of dawn (just like Hornblower) to look at the mountains of Spain, saw gliding silently close alongside, a British destroyer – an inexpressibly moving sight in those troubled days. It was more moving still to read at a much later time of the heroic end of that destroyer in battle against overwhelming forces.

POINT 1: Battle with privateer luggers off Ushant. POINT 2: Parting company with East India convoy off Cape St Vincent; impressment of seamen. *Special Note:* Operations on the Spanish coast are indicated in Map 24. Following points are *after* the Battle of Rosas. POINT 3: Hornblower taken by Colonel Caillard by coach from Rosas. POINT 4: Escape of the party from their escort. POINT 5: Château of Graçay. POINT 6: Briare: first camp. POINT 7: Nantes: capture of *Witch of Endor*. POINT 8: Noirmoutier: battle with shore boats. POINT 9: Meeting with Channel Fleet.

Map 23

General Map of Hornblower's Operations

- – → Track of *Sutherland*
- - - → Hornblower's journey by land
- ·········· Trip by boat down the Loire
- ← ·· ← Track of *Witch of Endor*

ENGLAND

London
Portsmouth • Dover
Plymouth Calais

Le Havre

FRANCE

Ushant
① Brest

Nantes
⑨ Angers
Beaugency
Moine Orléans Sully
Tours Blois Gien
⑦ Saumur Loire Chaumont ⑤ ⑥ Briare
⑧ Vienne Langeais ④ *Chateau of Graçay*
Noirmoutier Nevers

Moulins

Clermont-Ferrand
Issoire

Bay of

Biscay

Bordeaux

Cape
Finisterre

Cette
Toulon
See Map 24 Sigean
for details Perpignan
of action in Llanza
Chapters 9 ③ Rosas
to 20 of Palamos
Ship of Barcelona
the Line

SPAIN

Mediterranean Sea

②
Cape
St.Vincent
Gibraltar

STATUTE MILES
0   100   200

0   100   200
NAUTICAL MILES

Samuel H. Bryant

Map 24 * SHIP OF THE LINE
Chapters 9 to 20 * July to October, 1810

East Coast of Spain and
South Coast of France

THEY call this the Costa Brava, and there are villas for rent where Hornblower landed his guns at POINT 10, and painters set up their easels above the cliff where Hornblower had to climb for his life. The barges that chug along the lagoons are motorized now, but they are still manned by families just as was the one that Hornblower burned at POINT 5. Sudden gales like the one that dismasted the *Pluto* still come roaring down out of the mountains, and the tourist can stand on Cape Creux and look out over the sea where the *Sutherland* dragged her to safety at POINT 9. The holiday-maker luxuriating in the sunshine at POINT 14 may perhaps spare a moment's sympathy for the heartbroken Hornblower surrendering his ship in the bay – but not too much sympathy, because it was from here that he set out on the journey that was to carry him from mere distinction to resounding glory.

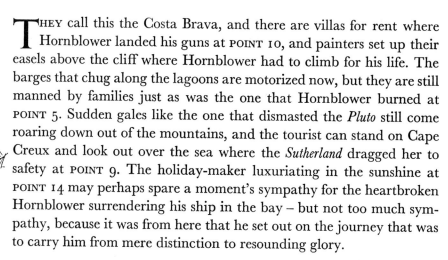

POINT 1: Palamos Point rendezvous with *Caligula*. POINT 2: Cape Creux: capture of *Amelie*. POINT 3: Llansa: storming of the battery. POINT 4: Port Vendres: cutting out expedition. POINT 5: Lagoon de Vic: burning of coaster. POINT 6: Arens de Mar: encounter with Colonel Villena. POINT 7: Bombardment of troops on coast road. POINT 8: Rendezvous with flagship. POINT 9: Storm off Cape Creux: *Pluto* dismasted. POINT 10: Silva de Mar: landing of siege artillery. POINT 11: Sights *Cassandra*: French fleet in sight. POINT 12: Position of remainder of British Squadron. POINT 13: Action between *Sutherland* and French fleet begins. POINT 14: Battle ends.

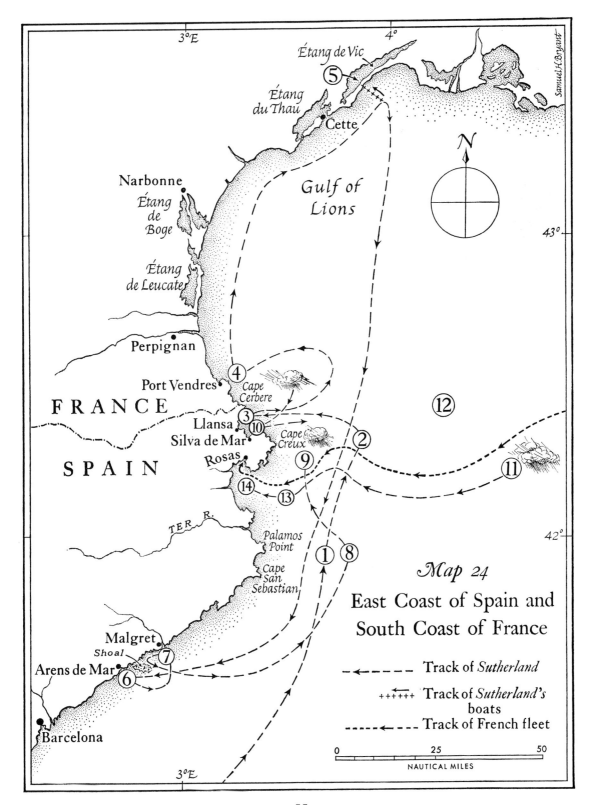

3°E

4°

Étang de Vic

⑤

Étang
du Thau

Cette

Narbonne

Étang
de
Boge

Gulf of
Lions

N

43°

Étang
de Leucate

Perpignan

FRANCE

Port Vendres

④

Cape
Cerbere

③
⑩

Llansa

Silva de Mar

Cape
Creux

②

⑫

SPAIN

Rosas

⑨

⑭

⑬

⑪

TER R.

Palamos
Point

42°

①

⑧

Cape
San
Sebastian

Map 24

East Coast of Spain and
South Coast of France

Malgret

Shoal

⑦

Arens de Mar

⑥

— — — ← — — Track of *Sutherland*

++++++ ← Track of *Sutherland's*
boats

Barcelona

- - - - ← - - - Track of French fleet

0   25   50

NAUTICAL MILES

3°E

Samuel H. Bryant

Map 25 * THE COMMODORE
Chapters 6 to 16 * May to July, 1812

The Baltic

THE strategical situation in the Baltic has changed radically since Hornblower ranged its length and breadth. As late as the Crimean War the British and French Navies had no difficulty in penetrating here and maintaining themselves, and even during the early years of the present century Admiral Fisher dreamed of landing a British expeditionary force on the coast of Pomerania, somewhere near POINT 2. The perfecting of the underwater mine and the cutting of the Kiel Canal made it certain – even before the development of air power – that Britain's superior navy would not be able to repeat Hornblower's exploits. Students of 'it might have been' may find diversion in estimating the effect of a powerful Russian Navy based on Kronstadt in 1914 or in 1941; more serious students may find profit in considering the problems of the command of the Baltic at the present day.

POINT 1: Sighting of *Maggie Jones*. POINT 2: *Lotus* sights *Blanche Fleur*. POINT 3: Meeting with Lord Wychwood. POINT 4: Interview with the Czar. POINT 5: Meeting with *Clam*.

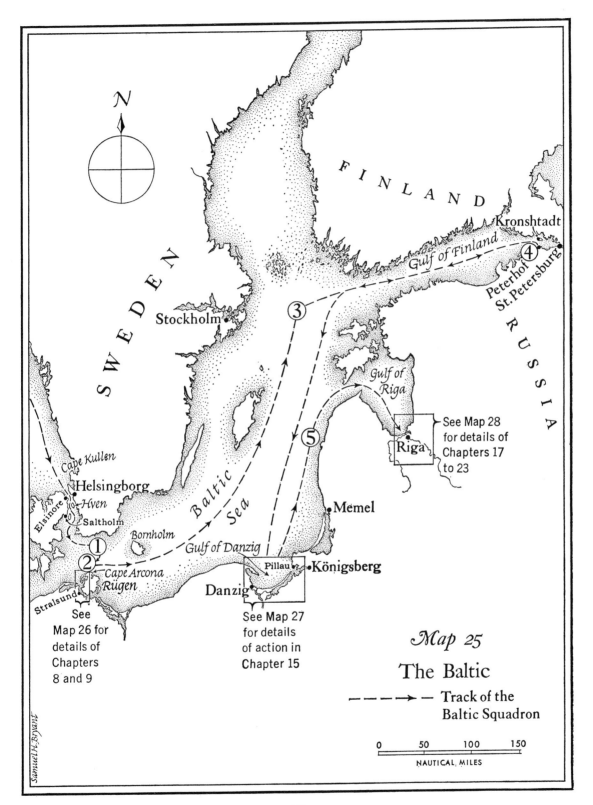

N

F I N L A N D

Kronshtadt

Gulf of Finland

④

Peterhof
St. Petersburg

S W E D E N

R U S S I A

Stockholm

③

Gulf of
Riga

See Map 28
for details of
Chapters 17
to 23

⑤

Riga

Cape Kullen

Helsingborg

Hven

Baltic

Memel

Elsinore

Saltholm

Sea

Bornholm

①

Gulf of Danzig

②
Cape Arcona
Rügen

Pillau
Königsberg

Stralsund

Danzig

See
Map 26 for
details of
Chapters
8 and 9

See Map 27
for details
of action in
Chapter 15

Map 25

The Baltic

— — — ▶ — Track of the
Baltic Squadron

0   50   100   150

NAUTICAL MILES

Samuel H. Bryant

57

Map 26 ∗ THE COMMODORE
Chapters 8 and 9 ∗ May, 1812
Bomb Vessels' Action off Rügen

THE Royal Navy made persistent use of bomb vessels during the Napoleonic Wars, but seldom with much success, and frequently with no success at all, as in the attacks on the French invasion flotillas in 1804. But a considerable number were retained in commission, not so much because (in the way that the White Knight carried a mousetrap on his horse) they might be useful sometime, but rather because their existence compelled the enemy to be constantly on guard in case they should appear over the horizon. Hornblower's bomb ketches were presented with the ideal opportunity when the *Blanche Fleur* took refuge behind Hiddensoe. There she thought she was safe even though her masts were visible; her movements were restricted by shoals, and there were no batteries near enough to protect her. Lateral observation of the fall of the shells made her destruction simple and rapid. The opportunity was there; Hornblower could be trusted to make the most of it.

POINT 1: *Raven* intercepts *Blanche Fleur* and then runs aground. POINT 2: *Blanche Fleur*'s anchorage. POINT 3: *Clam*'s position during firing. POINT 4: *Harvey*'s position during firing. POINT 5: *Moth*'s position during firing. POINT 6: *Lotus*'s position during firing. POINT 7: *Nonsuch*'s position during firing.

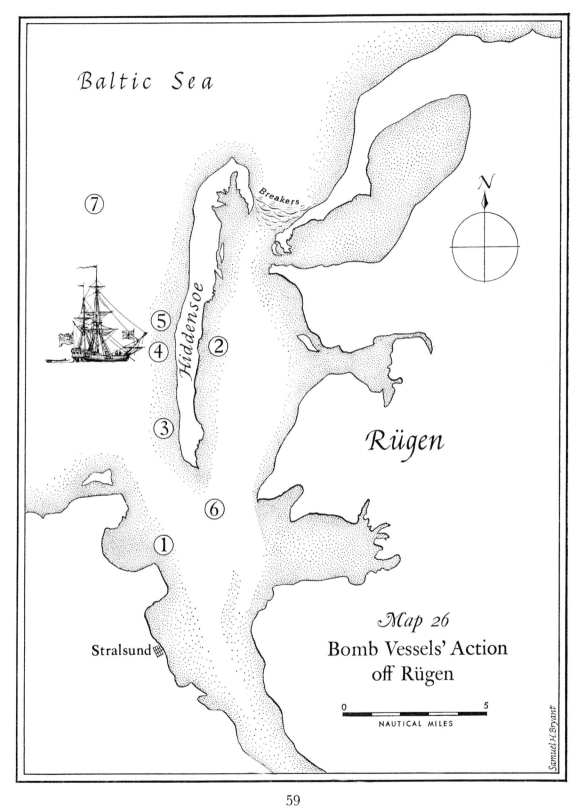

Baltic Sea

⑦

Breakers

Hiddensoe

⑤
④
③
②

⑥

①

Rügen

Stralsund

N

Map 26
Bomb Vessels' Action
off Rügen

0   5
NAUTICAL MILES

Samuel H.Bryant

Map 27 * THE COMMODORE
Chapter 15 * June, 1812

Action of the Boats in the Gulf of Danzig

IN EVERY land campaign involving large forces and long distances supplies had to be water-borne until the coming of railways and the internal combustion engine. Horse-drawn road transport was simply insufficient when a large army had to be maintained. Marlborough's campaigns, and the Wagram campaign of 1809, assume a new aspect, when studied in relation to communications by river and canal, and the old description of Spain as a country where small armies are beaten and large armies starve is really a comment on the absence of navigable rivers in the Peninsula. And Danzig was the main advance depot for a French Army invading Russia – it was the terminus of the whole Vistula system which tapped, with only a short land haul, the systems of the Elbe and the Oder as well. Hence the importance of Danzig, to which attention was even called in 1939. Hornblower's attack here was more difficult to guard against than some, because he was perfectly prepared to lose his ships' boats, which confused the defence, in the same way that precautions against assassination are likely to be ineffective when the assassin is perfectly reconciled to dying himself. It is to be assumed, although it is nowhere stated, that Hornblower later replaced the lost boats by local purchase or seizures.

POINT 1: Hornblower's false attack on Pillau. POINT 2: Entry of boats; see insert for details of boom. POINT 3: *Friedrich*, *Blitzer*, *Charlotte*, and *Ritterhaus* burned. POINT 4: *Weiss Ross* burned. POINT 5: Further destruction of shipping. POINT 6: Raiding boats abandoned. POINT 7: *Harvey* picks up crews.

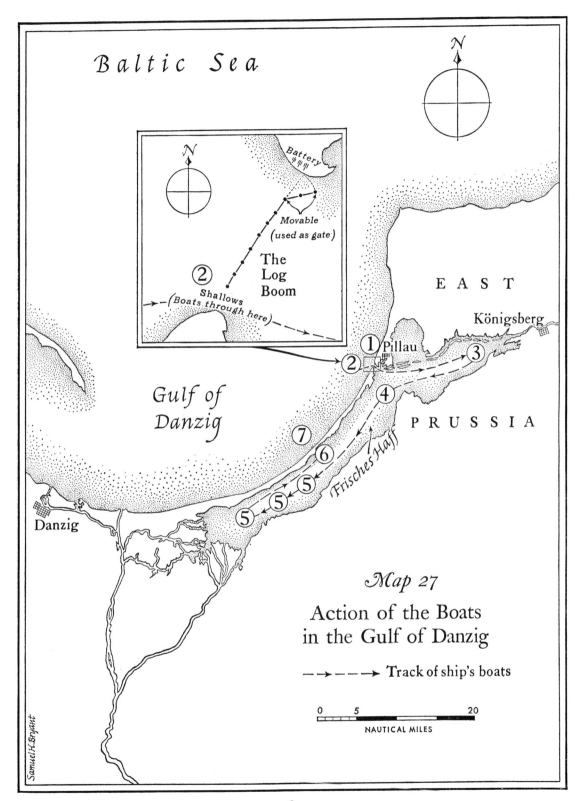

Baltic Sea

N

The Log Boom

N

Battery

Movable
(used as gate)

② Shallows
(Boats through here)

Gulf of
Danzig

EAST

Königsberg

① Pillau
②

③

④

PRUSSIA

⑦

⑥

⑤

⑤

⑤

Frisches Haff

Danzig

Map 27

Action of the Boats
in the Gulf of Danzig

– – →– – – → Track of ship's boats

0   5   20
NAUTICAL MILES

Samuel H. Bryant

Map 28 * THE COMMODORE

Chapters 17 to 23 * July to October, 1812

Riga

I<small>T</small> IS impossible to discover the sources from which Hornblower's biographer drew his account of the operations conducted here; the student is almost tempted to believe he drew on his imagination. Yet the broad outline is correct. Macdonald's advance on St Petersburg (where so far the name of Lenin had never been mentioned) was halted on the Dvina River at Riga; the Napoleonic forces invading Russia undoubtedly included unwilling contingents of Spaniards and Portuguese; and it was during the retreat from Riga that the first great defection took place – that of the Prussians – from the Napoleonic cause. But it was not until the publication of *The Commodore* that Hornblower's part in the vital political moves of the period was established, and if the student is willing to accept this account, he should find little trouble in believing in the other exploits of Hornblower and his squadron.

POINT 1: Middle ground anchorage. POINT 2: Capture of Major Jussey. POINT 3: Fight with barges carrying troops. POINT 4: Anchorage of bomb vessels during attack on French battery. POINT 5: Russian counter-attack: landing place.

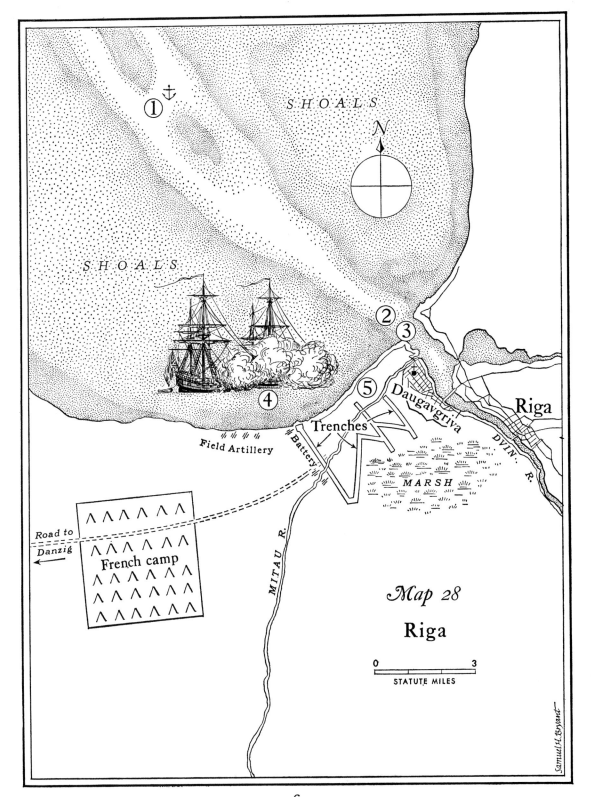

SHOALS

①⚓

N

SHOALS

②
③

④

⑤

Field Artillery

Trenches

Battery

Daugavgriva

Riga

DVIN. R.

MARSH

MITAU R.

Road to
Danzig

French camp

Map 28

Riga

0   3

STATUTE MILES

Samuel H. Bryant

Map 29 * LORD HORNBLOWER
Chapters 1 to 16 * October, 1813 to May, 1814
Normandy

THE Bay of the Seine is only too well remembered since 1944, but during the Napoleonic Wars it was infested by British small craft which suffered occasional losses as the result of vagaries of wind and tide. The defection of Le Havre, with the encouragement of a British force, is paralleled by the defection of Bordeaux at the same moment in history; the parallel is made closer still by the undeniable fact that the Duc d'Angoulême was apparently present in the two cities simultaneously, and the student is faced with a choice between history and Hornblower. It is worth noting that the *estacade* where Bush met his death at Caudebec has been rebuilt since the explosion, as the biographer once noted on a canoe trip down from Paris. But Captain Bush, from the manner of his death, has no grave, so that the biographer could only drop a random flower as a tribute to the memory of someone who, by association, had grown very dear to him.

POINT 1: First sighting of *Flame*. POINT 2: Captain Bush killed. POINT 3: News of the fall of the Empire.

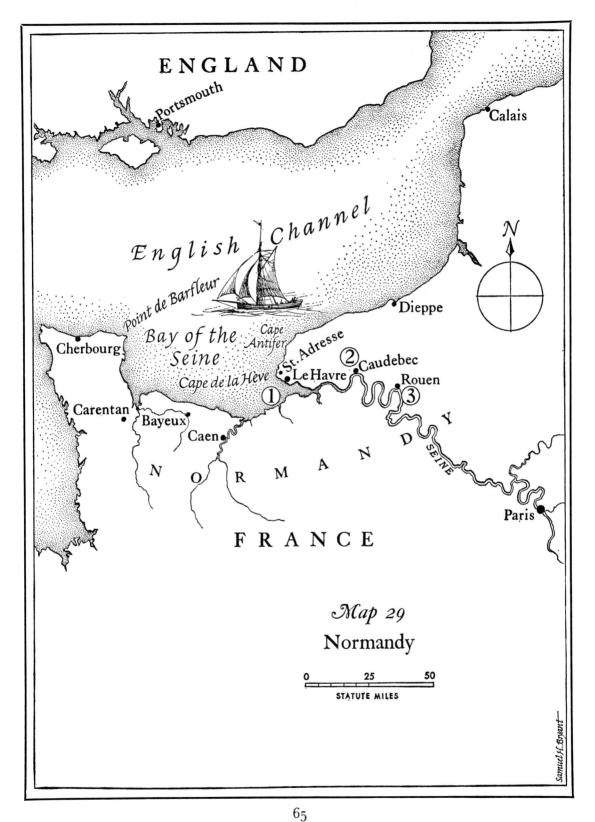

ENGLAND

Portsmouth

Calais

English Channel

Point de Barfleur

Dieppe

N

Cherbourg

Bay of the Seine

Cape Antifer

St.Adresse

② Caudebec

Rouen ③

Cape de la Hève

① Le Havre

Carentan

Bayeux

Caen

N O R M A N D Y

SEINE

Paris

F R A N C E

Map 29
Normandy

0   25   50
STATUTE MILES

Samuel H. Bryant

Map 30 * HORNBLOWER IN THE WEST INDIES

May, 1821 to October, 1823

General Map

CRUISE ships now are numerous in the waters where Hornblower once faced his problems; in Jamaica motor roads and bridges have replaced the tracks and the fords where Hornblower was escorted by the Bewildered Pirates, and fifteen minutes in a hired car will take the holiday-maker from Montego Bay to the cliff where he was held for ransom. Yet the Cockpit Country visible from that cliff is still an *imperium in imperio*, and hurricanes blow with all their old violence, and the events of 1962 proved that it was still possible for naval strength to be a dominant factor in time of peace in international disputes regarding the independence – or otherwise – of Caribbean territory. Finally (that is a comforting word for a writer to use on the last page) it should be pointed out that Hornblower was quite exceptional in attaining flag rank with only fifteen years seniority as a captain – every other captain on the list had to wait more than twenty in those piping years of peace. But if Hornblower had waited as long as that he would not have been an admiral at the time of Napoleon's death at St Helena, and St Elizabeth would have experienced her miracle in vain, while if ordinary rules had applied to him Hornblower would never have been Hornblower and this book and a dozen others would never have been written.

POINT 1: Meeting with *Daring*. POINT 2: Decision taken for new course. POINT 3: Second meeting with *Daring*. POINT 4: *Clorinda* and *Estrella del Sur*. POINT 5: The Bewildered Pirates. POINT 6: *Clorinda* and *Bride of Abydos*. POINT 7: Battle of Carabobo. POINT 8: Hurricane strikes.

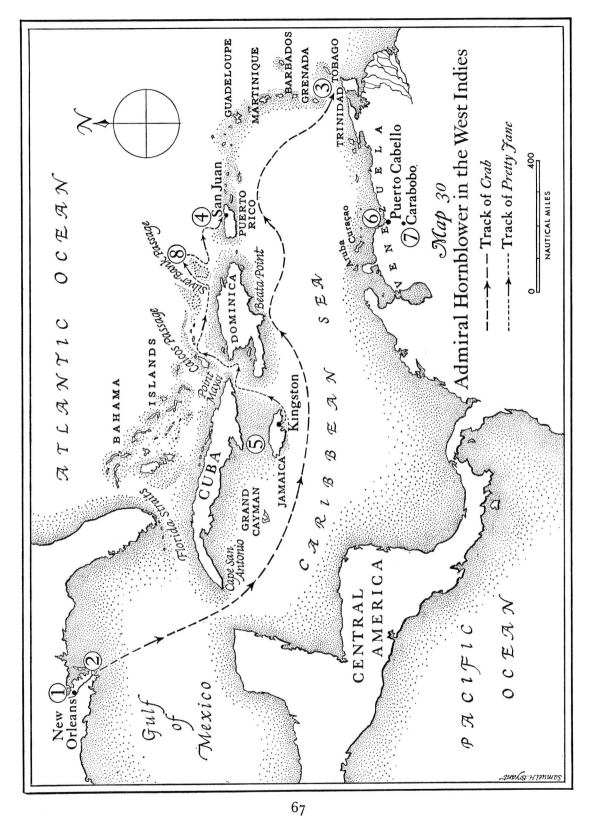

N

ATLANTIC OCEAN

BAHAMA ISLANDS

GUADELOUPE
MARTINIQUE
BARBADOS
GRENADA
③ TRINIDAD TOBAGO

San Juan
④ PUERTO RICO

Silver Bank Passage

Caicos Passage

Point Maysi

DOMINICA

Beata Point

CARIBBEAN SEA

Aruba
Curaçao
⑥ V E N E Z U E L A

Puerto Cabello
⑦ Carabobo

Map 30
Admiral Hornblower in the West Indies

------- Track of Crab
-------- Track of Pretty Jane

400

0

NAUTICAL MILES

CUBA

Cape San Antonio

GRAND CAYMAN

⑤ JAMAICA

Kingston

Florida Straits

New ①
Orleans ②

Gulf
of
Mexico

CENTRAL
AMERICA

PACIFIC OCEAN

Samuel H. Bryant

67

Some Personal Notes

Opposite is an example of the author's original manuscript. This particular material may be found in finished form on pages 77 to 78 of this book.

paper; what sets that forms these words? What is going on in my mind as I write them? I have no doubt that in my case it is a matter of *a series of* visualisations. Not two-dimensional, as if looking at a television screen; but three dimensional, perhaps, as if I were a thin invisible ghost walking about on a stage while a play is in actual performance. I can move about like, observe the actors from the back as well as the front, from *promptside* one side as well as *offsite prompt* the other, noticing their poses and their gestures & their speeches. One might almost call it four dimensional, because I am aware of the emotions & their motives as well. *So I record* what my judgment tells me are the essentials of the scene I am witnessing. I can run through a scene again like a Hollywood director in his chair in a projection room; *& when* I have finished with a scene I discard it and conjure up another one, *devised in my mind* put together all those weeks ago in the happy period of construction. It is really reporting, *for* almost all the invention has already been carried out, but it is surprising what a high degree of concentration *is apparent* during the process; *when* work is finished & I return to civilised life I am conscious of the same feeling of confusion — short lived, fortunately — as one feels when awakened from a vivid dream. And it is possible to lapse, to sneak back, or drift back, into the secret theatre & into the secret stage, from out of the workaday streets & the domestic life, so that *my rather* eyes me will distract or my bridge opponents exult in my lapses. (Almost all the invention has already been carried out, as I have said, but not quite all. A minor sort of invention is necessary at the work table — tactics rather than strategy. The words have to be chosen, the sentences devised, which most accurately & most economically — and most suitably — describe the scene I am witnessing. I have continually to ask myself if the paragraph I am writing will *conjure up the same* scene in the mind's eye of the reader, will make him equally aware of the emotions I am aware of. An awkward sentence may *bring* the reader back to reality, as a breaking stick may alert the feeding deer. An incorrectly worded sentence may convey an impression quite different from the one I wish to convey, so that each completed sentence has to *be* looked at objectively; the objective & the subjective have to work in unison — or at least alternately. (That is the great advantage of writing by hand instead of on a typewriter. Corrections are readily made, & not only to the sentence just *completed alterations*. Sometimes it is necessary to refer back a page or two, to *check* whether the object is *under one roof*, or two, or who it *or who made the last report*; one way or another every word is re-*read* once or twice, & the self-critical *most attitude* is naturally adopted then. On a hand-written page it is easy enough to substitute one word for another, or to transpose phrases with a ring & an arrow. Faced by a typewriter page, & the necessity of readjusting the carbon copies, it is possible to be lazy, to decide that the present wording will just do,

THERE are jellyfish that drift about in the ocean. They do nothing to seek out their daily food; chance carries them hither and thither, and chance brings them nourishment. Small living things come into contact with their tentacles, and are seized, devoured, and digested. Think of me as the jellyfish, and the captured victims become the plots, the stories, the outlines, the motifs – use whatever term you may consider best to describe the framework of a novel. In the ocean there are much higher forms of life than the jellyfish, and every human being in the ocean of humanity has much the same experience as every other human being, but some human beings are jellyfish and some are sharks. The tiny little food particles, the minute suggestive experiences, are recognized and seized by the jellyfish writer and are employed by him for his own specialized use.

We can go on with the analogy; once the captured victim is inside the jellyfish's stomach the digestive juices start pouring out and the material is transformed into a different protoplasm, without the jellyfish consciously doing anything about it until his existence ends with an abrupt change of analogy.

In my own case it happens that, generally speaking, the initial stimulus is recognized for what it is. The casual phrase dropped by a friend in conversation, the paragraph in a book, the incident observed by the roadside, has some special quality, and is accorded a special welcome. But, having been welcomed, it is forgotten, or at least ignored. It sinks into the horrid depths of my subconscious like a waterlogged timber into the slime at the bottom of a harbour, where it lies alongside others which have preceded it. Then, periodically – but by no means systematically – it is hauled up for examination along with its fellows, and, sooner or later, some timber is found with barnacles growing on it. Some morning when I am shaving, some evening when I am wondering whether my dinner calls for white wine or red, the original immature idea reappears in my mind, and it has grown. Nearly always it has something to do with what eventually will be the mid-point of a novel or a short story, and sometimes the growth is towards the end and sometimes towards the beginning. The casualty rate is high – some timbers grow no barnacles at all – but enough of them have progressed to keep me actively employed for more than forty years.

Examination completed, the timber is dropped back again into the slime, to be fished out every now and then until the barnacles are found to be quite numerous. That is when the plot is really beginning to take shape; that is when the ideas relating to it recur to me more and more often, so that they demand a greater and greater proportion of my attention as the days go by, until, in the end, the story might almost be described as an obsession, colouring my thoughts and influencing my actions and my behaviour. Generally some real work is called for at this stage, to clear up some mechanical difficulty. At some point in the plot it may be essential for the *Lydia* and the *Natividad* to be at the same place at the same time – what forces (other than pure coincidence) can bring this about? What has happened earlier that makes it quite inevitable? A different kind of inventiveness has to be employed here.

This sort of difficulty is sometimes cleared up in a peculiar and often gratifying fashion – I have known it to happen half a dozen times. I have been developing two different plots, both of them vaguely unsatisfactory, and then suddenly they have dovetailed together, like two separate halves of a jigsaw puzzle – the difficulties have vanished, the story is complete, and I am experiencing a special, intense pleasure, a glow of satisfaction – entirely undeserved – which is perhaps the greatest reward known to my profession.

2

So at last the construction is completed, the beginning and the end are determined upon, and all the intermediate steps (with occasional exceptions, one or two of which will be noticed later in this essay), so that all that remains is to write the thing. Please do not think that I am laying down rules for the writing of novels. Other writers employ other methods. Some novels are begun without planning; the writer's invention carries him on to an end which at first he does not foresee. Sometimes characters in a novel take charge while the novel is being written and insist on developments utterly unanticipated. Yet, even so, I believe that basically there is no essential difference of method. Writers who work in these ways are doing on paper what I prefer to do – or must do – in my mind before I start on the paper. Characters of mine who take charge do so during the preliminary thought; those developments are new barnacles on the timber.

Now, with regard to this construction; clearly there are two extremes in the matter of procedure. The writer may first think of the deed that is going to be done, and then ask himself who would be the most suitable – and most interesting – person to do that deed; on the other hand the writer may think of a character and then ask himself what would be a likely – and interesting – deed for that person to do. On the one hand no one can imagine that Jonathan Swift first thought of the character of Lemuel Gulliver and then thought of sending him to an island populated by a race of people six inches tall. Swift must have thought about Lilliput first, and then have developed the most suitable person to send there. Gulliver, with his shrewdness and simplicity, his knowledge of the world, and his ignorance – all quite human and believable – was the ideal person to observe and comment upon the cultures that he encountered. Without Gulliver the *Travels* would be pointless fantasy; without the *Travels* Gulliver would still be someone to be reckoned with; but all the same he owes his existence to the *Travels*.

There is a magnificent, an awe-inspiring example of this in *Hamlet*. It is hard to believe that Shakespeare conjured up that complex character and then arbitrarily made him a dispossessed prince in Denmark. It seems quite obvious that Shakespeare thought of (or read of) the situation first – the incest, the murder, the dispossession – and then built up Hamlet in his mind as the most interesting person to face the situation, alone, without a confidant, and hampered by his own complexities.

The most convenient example of the other method of approach, in which the character comes first, that I can think of, is *Madame Bovary*. I feel quite sure that Flaubert knew a great deal about her before he decided upon what she was going to do, and that he built her up in his mind before making the discovery that she was a suitable person through whom to exploit the 'realism' that attracted him after the *Temptation of Saint Anthony*. Then that discovery naturally dictated the things that would happen to her, the deeds she did; the story came into existence because of Madame Bovary, and not the other way about.

<h1 style="text-align:center">3</h1>

IN any case, whatever the method of construction, the book still has to be written. The ideas formed in the mind have to be fixed on paper. First of all, a start has to be made – that statement of the obvious is justified by the magnitude of the truth it contains. The happy-go-lucky methods of the jellyfish have to be abandoned for the diligence of the ant and the endurance of the mule. For me personally, the change of state occasioned by beginning to write is abrupt and violent. It is the difference between standing at the top of the toboggan slide and starting the descent. It is taking the plunge, swallowing the pill, walking through the door marked 'Abandon Hope'. It means giving up the pleasant life of contemplation for a period of the hardest and most unrelenting work, because (as experience has long taught me) it is hard work, exhausting work. I am held back by the thought of what I am leaving behind as well as by the thought of what I am entering into. At some moment I have to sit myself at my worktable, write the figure '1' at the top of the first page on my pad, and then begin the opening paragraph; that is when the toboggan is pushed off, and there is no going back.

There are various devices to bring this about; the most usual one is to tell my publisher that I am contemplating a novel and to promise a date for delivery – promise it solemnly, with no ifs or perhapses. I have done this maybe twenty times, and I have never broken one of those promises. To do so would be like a reformed drunkard taking his first glass of whisky. My last safeguard against idleness would be down. Contemplation of the rapidly changing dates on the calendar, calculation of the number of days left to me in which to keep my promise, drive me into action sooner or later – not sooner, but later.

4

For me there is no other way of writing a novel than to begin at the beginning and to continue to the end, and that is not quite the statement of the obvious as it might appear. Other people have other methods; I have heard of novels started in the middle, at the end, written in patches to be joined together later, but I have never felt the slightest desire to do this. The end is in my mind, of course, and so are the intermediate passages, and I rush forward, leaping from one solid foothold to the next, like Eliza leaping from one cake of ice to the next on the Ohio River.

There is still need to think and to plan, but on a different scale, and along different lines. The work is with me when I wake up in the morning; it is with me while I eat my breakfast in bed and run through the newspaper, while I shave and bathe and dress. It is the coming day's work which is occupying my thoughts; the undemanding routine activities permit – encourage – my mind to work on the approaching difficulties, to solve the tactical problems which arise in the execution of the strategical plan. So, the day's work is clear, usually, in my mind as I stand screwing up my resolution to begin again. Then I find myself in my workroom, uncapping my fountain pen and pulling my pad towards me and glancing down the paragraphs written yesterday, and instantly I am swept away into composition.

Yet, surprisingly perhaps, it is hard work, exacting and exhausting work. For me (I know many novelists who feel differently) the pleasure to be found in the act of composition is overlaid by the physical and mental fatigue that it occasions. From one point of view I would rather be in the dentist's chair. This is largely the result of the defect in my temperament which will not allow

76

me to work slowly. I have never learned restraint in all this time. I cannot bear to rest or to wait. Once started, the day's work must be done, and done it is, perhaps in an hour, perhaps in three hours, but always when it is finished there is the sick, weary, flat feeling of exhaustion. There is no pleasure left in life; I am drained and empty, and the rest of my day is lived by a different creature, mindless and spineless, who is creeping back to a resemblance to humanity only as the evening draws to a close.

It is the knowledge that this is going to happen to me that makes the initial plunge into work such a difficult step to take. But the reluctance that shows itself each morning afterwards is more easily overcome. First of all there is the knowledge gained by experience that one day's postponement is like the one drink of a drunkard. Tomorrow's postponement is easier still, and when I finally emerge from my bout of laziness three weeks have passed by, and the after-effects are so unpleasant that nowadays I have learned to maintain a firm front. Another factor is routine; after a few days' work I have slipped into the habit of starting work at the earliest possible moment each day, to such an extent that much as I dislike the thought of work, I dislike even more the present feeling of not having worked – and there is no stronger expression than that. And lastly there is the temperamental desire to finish the thing, not merely to rid myself of this burden that I am carrying, but in order to gratify my curiosity. There are certain things ahead to be done, there are certain moods to express, there are difficult corners to turn. Will the plans I have made prove adequate? Will I be able to find the right words to express the feeling I wish to convey? There is only one way to find out, and that is to go on writing.

5

SITTING at a table writing words on paper; what is it that forms those words? What is going on in my mind as I write them? I have no doubt that in my case it is a matter of a series of visualizations. Not two-dimensional, as if looking at a television screen; three-dimensional, perhaps, as if I were a thin, invisible ghost walking about on a stage while a play is in actual performance. I can move where I like, observe the actors from the back as well as the front, from prompt side as well as opposite prompt, noting their poses and their concealed gestures and their speeches. One might almost call it four-dimensional, because I am aware of their emotions and their motives as well. So I record what my judgment tells me are the essentials of the scene I am witnessing. I can run through a scene again, like a Hollywood director in his chair in a projection room, and when I have finished with a scene I discard it and conjure up another one, devised in my mind all those weeks ago in the happy period of construction. It is really reporting, for almost all the invention has already been carried out, but it is surprising what a high degree of concentration is necessary during the process; when the day's work is finished and I return to civilized life I am conscious of the same feeling of confusion – short-lived, fortunately – as one feels when awakened from a vivid dream. And it is possible to lapse, to sneak back, or drift back, into the secret theatre and on to the secret stage, from out of the workaday streets and the domestic life, so that my dinner partner eyes me with distrust or my bridge opponents exult in my lapses.

Almost all the invention has already been carried out, as I have just said, but not quite all. A minor sort of invention is necessary at the worktable – tactics rather than strategy. The words have to be chosen, the sentences devised, which most accurately and most economically – and most suitably – describe the scene I am witnessing. I have to ask myself continually if the paragraph I am writing will conjure up the same scene in the mind's eye of the reader, will make him equally aware of the emotions I am aware of. An awkward sentence may bring the reader back to reality, as a breaking stick may alert the feeding deer. An incorrectly worded sentence may convey an impression quite different from the one I wish to convey, so that each completed sentence has to be looked at objectively; the objective and the subjective have to work in unison – or at least alternately.

That is the great advantage of writing by hand instead of on a typewriter. Alterations are readily made, and not only in the sentences just completed. Sometimes it is necessary to refer back a page or two, to check whether the ship is under one reef or two, or who it was made the last report; one way or another every word is reread once or twice, and the self-critical mood is naturally adopted then. On a handwritten page it is easy enough to substitute one word for another, or to transpose phrases with a ring and an arrow. Faced by a typewritten page, and the necessity to re-align the carbon copies, it is possible to be lazy, to decide that the present wording will just do, even though conscience says otherwise. The self-critical impulse is easily enough diverted in any case, because it is distasteful to follow it, to face the fact that I have written something incorrectly, that my judgment has been at fault, or simply that I have been careless. To recognize my imperfections comes hard; to force myself to look for them comes harder still, but it is necessary – just as an ugly woman has to force herself to examine objectively her image in the mirror to see what can best be done about it, even if she hates what she sees.

So time goes on; each day brings its quota of words, its finished pages, and with each day the increasing desire to have the thing finished grows stronger. I have learned not to indulge it. Unpleasant experience has taught me that to work on and on through the day and to finish a prodigious amount at a sitting is ill-judged. (Remember, I am only discussing my own methods; other people successfully use other methods.) Next day I am sick and bone-weary and I *cannot* work. Not even the most objective and impersonal analysis of my motives brings me to the conclusion that I am being influenced by plain laziness, by mere distaste for exertion. It is *impossible* for me to work, and my loss today is greater than my gain of yesterday. In consequence I have to remain orderly and methodical, and there are few people in this world naturally less orderly and methodical than I am. I have to plod along from day to day, from the beginning to the end, even though my instinct is to act as if the beginning were a forest fire and the end some safe refuge of desert country.

Three months – four months – something in between those two limits, and then at last it is finished. There is no pleasure, even, in writing the final word; my mind is too numb to feel anything of the sort. Not even relief; for the next thing to do is read the completed typescript – a long-suffering secretary has been following me up, two or three days behind me, and within a day or two the final pages are typed. Naturally I have glanced at the typescript during the progress of the work, but now I have to read the whole thing through – out of curiosity, perhaps; I can think of no other reason. And there it is. The ugly woman, having completed her make-up, can now study the final result, of course with disappointment. Can a finished book ever be as good as the book the writer dreamed of before he started writing it? I cannot believe that to be possible, for obvious reasons; certainly it has never happened to me. Luckily the numbness and weariness take the edge off the disappointment. I am too tired to feel it deeply. And the mental attitude changes a little, so that I can reach the decision to send the typescript off to a publisher. Trying to be as objective as I can, I am ready to agree, reluctantly, that the book is as good as I could ever make it – there is nothing I can do to improve it. The shortcomings that displease me are my own, and I have lived with my own shortcomings long enough to be callous about them. By the time I have finished a book I am callous about pretty nearly everything. Let it go – let me come back into the normal world which I left three months ago. Those three months have been devoid of every ordinary reaction; as far as my daily life is concerned I might as well have been under an anaesthetic.

7

YET my distaste for my own work lingers on surprisingly. A father looking down at his first-born for the first time may experience a sense of shock, but he generally recovers from it rapidly enough; after a day or two he thinks it is a very wonderful baby indeed. My life would be happier if I reacted in the same way towards my books – the odd thing being that even as it is there are very few people who lead a happier life than mine, despite all the feelings that I have just been describing. I must be like the princess who felt the pea through seven mattresses; each book is a pea. Inevitably, the proofs start coming in, set after set of them, English proofs, American proofs, serial proofs, and every set has to be read carefully and objectively for the literal mistakes it contains – different ones for each set. I approach the first set with distaste and the fourth or fifth set with horror. By the fourth or fifth reading the imperfections have grown huge in my mind; I feel, quite seriously, that no one will ever bother with this nonsense.

Because of this feeling, favourable reviews and kindly comments by friends do not bring the satisfaction I expected in the days when I first wrote. People who say or write nice things about my books must clearly be people with no perception whatever and their opinions not worth consideration. Luckily, the acute phase of this trouble does not last long. A feeling of amused tolerance replaces the distaste, and all troubles are forgotten in the delicious pleasure of not being exhausted each day. To recognize my children when I meet them in the street; to seek out once more that elusive difference (unnoticeable while I am working) between WHITSTABLES and COLCHESTERS; to welcome the dawn as an old friend whether I am on my way home or on my way out; to bathe in the euphoria of having energy to waste; to undertake some of the myriad projects (unconnected with novel writing) left neglected during this little death – these are things that (thanks to my profession) I enjoy far more keenly than less fortunate persons.

8

AND, almost unnoticed, the next story begins to creep into this delightful life. The serpent enters into Eden, but without arousing apprehension, even when, eventually, it is recognized for what it is. There are the moments of solid satisfaction at each advance in construction, there is the pleasure experienced (greater, rather than less, in being entirely undeserved) when, during the course of an idle morning, the discovery is made that an awkward corner has been turned; these are all the innocent, and yet astonishingly acute, joys of creation to add to the pleasure of being alive and in Eden. Perhaps it is the best life that anyone could ever lead.

Even when serious work has to be done on the construction, when the final phase is reached, there is still no cloud to obscure the sun. This new book, if it ever comes to be written, will be as nearly perfect as any book can be. It will be easy enough to make sure that the imperfections that disfigure its predecessor will not occur in this one. And if ever I set about writing it I shall have some sense. I will work slowly and stay cheerful and free from fatigue. Perhaps this experience will be much better than the last – I can be sure that nothing could be worse, anyway. And if I delay any longer, with this story demanding expression, Eden will not remain quite the same Eden. And so I walk into my workroom, uncapping my fountain pen, and the doors of Eden slam behind me, not to reopen until I have suffered the whole cycle again.

9

I CAN remember how Hornblower started. It was buying a book that prepared the slime into which the first waterlogged timber would be dropped. The *Naval Chronicle;* this was a magazine published monthly from about 1790 to 1820, written largely by naval officers for naval officers. There were three volumes in a second-hand bookshop – six issues in each, bound together – and I bought them in 1927 because I was looking for books to supply a library for a small boat on which I was going to live for several months together. They were biggish books in small print, crammed with facts, and (within limits) covering a wide range of subjects – ideal for the purpose. The fact that they were of nautical interest gave them added attraction, although that was not the decisive factor. I might possibly have bought books about banking methods or law – in that case would I later have found myself committed to write a novel-cycle about banking? I suppose that is possible, but I cannot believe it.

Those volumes of the *Naval Chronicle* were read and reread during the months that followed, and perhaps I absorbed some of the atmosphere; certainly I became very familiar with the special mental attitude of naval officers at that time regarding various aspects of their profession.

And in one of the volumes was the actual text of the Treaty of Ghent signed in December, 1814, making peace between the United States and England. The general terms can be found in any standard history, but for me there is a special attraction about detail – how these things were actually expressed at the time, the exact wording, the moods hinted at in the words. Here was Article Two, defining when the war should legally end; in the North Atlantic, twelve days after the ratification, the interval increasing to forty days for the Baltic and so on up to a hundred and twenty days for distant parts of the Pacific.

This was an interesting illustration of the difficulties of communication, and gave rise to odd trains of thought. If you captured a ship off Java one hundred and nineteen days after the ratification, that ship was yours, but if you captured a ship one hundred and twenty-one days after ratification you had to hand it back. And if the capture took place after exactly one hundred and twenty days what happened then? And if it happened on the wrong side of the International Dateline? There were possibilities of all sorts of disappointments and heartburnings along these lines. Down into the slime went the waterlogged timber.

10

In any case, there was more material for the subconscious to work on in dealing with the situation of the man who has to make unaided decisions. The man alone; he may have technical help, he may even have friends, but as regards the crisis he is facing he can only act on his own judgment, and in case of failure he has only himself to blame. The murderer, who, having committed his crime, dare confide in nobody and must plan his future actions without assistance, is one example of the single-handed man; at the ripe age of twenty-three I had dealt exhaustively (so I thought) with a murderer and his problems, but there was still a great deal not yet said regarding the Man Alone. There was the terrifying perfection of Hamlet; but in the world there are uses to be found for candles even after arc lights have been invented.

This Man Alone – the captain of a ship, and more especially of a ship of war, was very much alone in the days before radiotelegraphy. A captain like one of those I had been reading about – barnacles were growing apace on the waterlogged timber.

There was another interest at this time, besides the *Naval Chronicle* and the allied reading which it had led me into. This was the Peninsular War. Sir Charles Oman had just finished his *History* in several large volumes – one of the best histories, and certainly one of the best military histories ever written. The painstaking care it displayed left me in awe; the myriad details enchanted me so much that I had written two military novels dealing with the period. Even though those novels were now behind me, and other work occupied my attention, there were still lingering memories. The character of Wellington himself was fascinating – and he was certainly an example during the Peninsular War of the Man Alone, although not quite of the type that was taking form in my mind. Also in his family had occurred one of the most resounding scandals in a scandal-ridden age; his brother's wife had eloped with the cavalry general who was later to become Marquis of Anglesey. The repercussions of that elopement spread far through history; that was very interesting.

Another detail that held my notice was quite unrelated. When the war was at its height, and the Spanish Government was fighting for its life against the Napoleonic armies, Spanish troops were actually withdrawn from the struggle and sent across the Atlantic to repress a rebellion that had broken out in Mexico. The Spanish-American empire was beginning to fall to pieces, and communications were long and difficult. And barnacles were still growing on those sunken timbers, attaching themselves almost unnoticed while my conscious mind was at work on novels like *The African Queen* and *The General*.

II

Now came a coincidence, although its connection with Hornblower was not at that time apparent in the least. Hugh Walpole, whom I had never seen, nor spoken to, nor corresponded with, was at work in Hollywood; the Hollywood of the new talkies, at the height of its power and pride and wealth and insolence. Walpole was asked, inevitably, who among the young writers in England showed promise and might be useful in handling this new medium; it happened that he gave my name. So a letter arrived for me asking if, were I to be invited to come to work in Hollywood, would I accept the invitation? Would I cross the Atlantic and visit those outlandish United States? Would I commit myself to working in that Hollywood about which such fantastic tales circulated? If, at that moment, some novel had held me in thrall I might well have refused, but as it was I was momentarily preoccupied with a very minor interest – a mere marionette theatre. In any case it was common knowledge that Hollywood promised much and delivered little. I wrote back saying that I would accept the invitation if it came, but I was quite sure that the invitation would never come. Yet it came, charged with all the desperate urgency of Hollywood, so that after forty-eight hours of active visa-seeking and desperate packing I found myself sailing for New York in the old *Aquitania*.

Details of that first period of work in Hollywood are of no importance as regards this present discussion, except from one point of view. It has always been my experience that ideas do not form themselves in my mind when I am leading what might be thought a contemplative life, doing nothing whatever. Activity, violent interests outside a life of writing, a crisis twice a week and a catastrophe every Saturday, with neither the leisure nor the strength to do any serious thinking – a few weeks of that sort of life and when a breathing spell arrives I make the gratifying discovery that the subconscious ideas have developed and fresh barnacles have grown on the submerged timbers. And the newcomer to Hollywood in those days faced new crises twice a day, not merely twice a week; it needed experience to discover that not one of the crises mattered, and that emotion ran only skin deep. Encountering a new culture, seeing new sights, breathing a different air – and goaded into ever-fresh activity by a natural curiosity – I certainly had no time for contemplation.

The final crisis was personal to me. After going along from one job to another I found myself engaged by Irving Thalberg – perhaps the most prominent Hollywood personality at that time – to work on a screen play about Charles Stewart Parnell. No two people on earth, perhaps, were less suited to work together than Thalberg and me; and perhaps the spirit of Parnell did nothing to soften any personal difficulties. Then, idly, I noticed the announcement of the sailing next day from San Pedro of the Swedish ship *Margaret Johnson*, of the Johnson Line, with freight and passengers for Central American ports, the Panama Canal, and England. An idle reading, perhaps, but it brought about an immediate change. There was the instant realization that I wanted no more of Hollywood, that I never wanted to work under instruction again, that I wanted my freedom, that I was passionately anxious to see England once more. (I feel compelled at this point to interrupt the narrative by mentioning that since that time I have managed to work in Hollywood, without active unhappiness at least.) But this was the moment for action. Within the hour I was a free man, having tendered my resignation comfortably ahead of dismissal. Before the day was over I had engaged a passage, and, remarkably, had settled my income tax with Internal Revenue. And before the next day was well advanced I was standing on the deck of the *Margaret Johnson* watching the United States sink below the horizon.

12

THAT was an extraordinarily happy time. Central America in those days could only be visited by ship – such ships as the *Margaret Johnson* herself – and this was the time of the coffee harvest. We wandered about from one little harbour to another, from one open roadstead to the next, picking up fifty bags of coffee here and a hundred there, and if the harbour facilities – the rickety pier or the battered old lighters – were already pre-empted by another ship we dropped anchor and waited without impatience. When we steamed into the

Gulf of Fonseca to find the port of La Unión already occupied, and had to anchor beside the island of Meanguera, the captain took advantage of the delay to put the lifeboats through their annual test; and when the big motor lifeboat was in the water the first mate and I persuaded him to let us go off in it on a long voyage of exploration into the inner recesses of the Gulf.

There were forgotten villages, lashed by the rain and roasted in the sun, where pathetic life moved on at a snail's pace, where old, old women squatted in the market place mutely offering for sale their entire stock in trade – a single egg held in a skinny hand. Back at sea again there were sudden violent storms that laid the *Margaret Johnson* well over on her beam ends, a hurricane wind that picked me up when I incautiously emerged on to the open deck and flung me twenty feet against the rail and very nearly through it. There was blazing sun, and volcanoes glowing at night, and the False Cross visible on the southern horizon. There was a civilized interval while passing through the Panama Canal, and then more beachcombing along the coast of the Caribbean.

For six weeks this went on, six weeks with nothing to do except to observe, to feel, and, vaguely, to think, while the tension that had built up in Hollywood gradually eased off. The captain was a shuffleboard enthusiast, an addict; for him shuffleboard was one of the important things in life, and he and I played hundreds and hundreds of games on the blazing upper deck – the *Margaret Johnson* had a long, easy roll, and there was a certain fascination about standing waiting to shove one's disc while keeping an eye out over the ship's side so as to pick exactly the right moment to send the disc slithering along on a curved path between two hostile discs laid as obstacles – with good timing the disc could be made to behave almost intelligently. Stabilizers have taken half the fun out of shuffleboard. All the same, shuffleboard made no extravagant demands on the brain; it provided healthy exercise for the body while keeping the mind just busy enough so that it could not act on its own account and the subconscious could have full play. Every now and then the results became evident as the submerged timbers revealed fresh barnacles.

That break-up of the Spanish-American Empire; twice at least while Spain was an ally of Bonaparte England had made common cause, disastrously, with malcontents in South America in the hope of detaching the Spanish colonies from the Spanish crown. It was odd to think of British forces fighting in Montevideo and Buenos Aires, but there had even been moments when the British flag flew in Manila and Java. And on the lost Pacific coast of Central America queer things could happen. Someone could set himself up as an independent, and in that enlightened country a leader could be an untrammelled tyrant, as the later history of the Central American republics amply proved. And a tyrant in that country? El Supremo began to take shape, and also began to dovetail in with the possibility of British support. Had not Nelson himself, as a young captain, nearly lost his life on some similar hare-brained expedition to the Mosquito Coast?

Nelson, of course, had been involved in the Nelson-Hamilton scandal which had preceded the Anglesey-Wellesley scandal. Did Wellington ever have a sister, and not a mere sister-in-law? Wellington's intensely interesting personal character would be more interesting still in the female line, and I already knew enough about the influence of politics on naval careers to guess what part the Wellesley clan might play in a novel of the period; clearly (as was once said in another connection) if a Wellesley sister did not exist it would be necessary to invent one.

13

THE *Margaret Johnson* went out through the Mona Passage from the Caribbean into the Atlantic, and with that change – quite probably in consequence of it – the vital step in the construction was taken. That first faint hint remembered from years back, which had been calling attention to itself and demanding recognition and incorporation – the difficulty in olden days of disseminating the news that a war had ended and a peace begun – applied with special and peculiar force to a Central American situation. For the change in the attitude of Spain in 1808 was not only rapid but especially drastic. Bonaparte's attempt to set his brother on the throne of Spain turned every Spaniard overnight from an enemy of England into an enthusiastic ally; there were few examples in history of such an instant political change – war was generally preceded by a period of tension, and peace by a period of negotiation. The results of such a complete reversal could be especially dramatic in Central America if a British naval expedition there had first encouraged a separatist movement and then had to aid in suppressing it. My gloomy tyrant on the shores of the Gulf of Fonseca would have opportunities of revealing himself first as an ally and then as an enemy. The presence of Barbara Wellesley (I believe she had already been christened) would be susceptible to explanation and would not result from too wild a coincidence. The novel now had a beginning and an end, and – to drag in yet one more metaphor – with the identification of the keypiece the rest of the jigsaw puzzle fell into place, without further effort, to reveal the whole picture.

86

That was a moment of enormous satisfaction, as the *Margaret Johnson* headed into the trade winds northeastward across the Atlantic, and the long roll which had added so much interest to the games of shuffleboard was replaced by a shorter pitch-and-toss that altered their character. My character changed too; now I was Tom o'Bedlam, gradually becoming surrounded by dream figures more real than those of this world. Blandly abstracted, I lived the routine life of the ship without giving it a thought; my mind was now actively busy. When and how would the news of peace be received? What must be the attitude of the frigate's lieutenants one to another? How could the drama of such-and-such a situation be best expressed? The person who spoke to me at noontime with the result of the calculations of the ship's run would be mildly puzzled at my careless – almost deaf – reaction; he had summoned me out of an interview with El Supremo, possibly; I looked – I am sure – like a man awakened from a dream even though I had been pacing the deck, apparently normal. At least I refrained (unlike Gray's character) from muttering my wayward fancies aloud – self-consciousness inhibited that ultimate exhibition of abstraction, likely though it was, in my state of excitement.

14

THE Azores drew near; the trade winds dropped astern, and Hornblower began to develop a personality; to a large extent he was already formed by the necessities of the story. As in real life we are moulded both by heredity and environment, so in fiction characters must have certain qualities in order to be able to perform their destined parts, and then are given additional ones in order to make the necessary ones more believable, or to make the character himself more believable, or because he could not endure what he is to undergo without these additional qualities, or even – and ultimately – because these characteristics seem suitable, fitting, and right.

Hornblower was to be the Man Alone that I had sought. He had a definite task, or series of tasks, to perform in the course of this novel that I contemplated, but that task was only a part of a greater whole – while fighting El Supremo he was fighting for his country against the continental tyranny of Bonaparte. And then he had another task as well, one of much longer duration, and perhaps of greater importance to him, and of greater importance still to me. Wars could reasonably be expected to end; Bonaparte might reasonably be expected to fall – at any rate such highly desired possibilities were at least possibilities, but Hornblower's other struggle would go on as long as he was to live, for it was the struggle with himself. He was to be self-critical. Just as no man is supposed to be a hero to his own valet, so Hornblower could not be a hero to his own self. He would be too cynical about his own motives, too aware of his own weaknesses, ever to know content; and he would have to be a man of considerable character so that, even though despairing – hopeless – he could maintain this struggle with himself and not subside into self-satisfaction or humility.

So now a great deal about Hornblower was settled. He was the captain of a British frigate – not of a ship of the line, for naval policy demanded that ships of the line should be kept in fleets, or at least squadrons, and not dispersed in units. Nor would Hornblower be captain of a mere sloop, for a sloop would be too small for the task contemplated. This gave a measure of his seniority, for as a general rule the more senior the captain the larger his ship. Hornblower would be likely to have from three to ten years' seniority as captain. He was not a man of blue blood – that would over-simplify his affair with Lady Barbara – so that his promotions would have been due to merit and not to influence; giving additional force to this would be the fact that he had been entrusted with this single-handed mission – he was a man of mark to some modest extent. So that as his promotion had been comparatively prompt he would now be in his early thirties – a convenient age for his entanglement with Lady Barbara, whose elder brother was indisputably thirty-nine in 1808. A convenient age, too, because I was in my late thirties and could look down on my juniors with Olympian neutrality.

Incidentally, he would have to speak Spanish well, in order to save interminable trouble with interpreters while negotiating with El Supremo, and the need for a reasonable explanation of this ability tells us one thing about his professional past – he was at one time a prisoner of war in Spain.

He was a married man, of course – otherwise there would be no difficulty with Lady Barbara; and what had already been settled went a long way towards fixing the character of the wife, about whom something had to be known, although she would make no personal appearance. She was hardly likely to be sensitive, or intelligent or experienced, because if she had been she might be expected to have done something to loosen some of the knots Hornblower was tied up in. Likewise, she was a woman of the people, for if she were of blue blood Hornblower's approach to Lady Barbara would be simplified. It was lucky that there would be no need to explain how a man like Hornblower had come to marry a woman like this Maria; the reader could be expected to know that mismarriages happened.

88

Now for the rest of Hornblower. He must be perceptive and imaginative, for otherwise he would not see the things and the possibilities that were going to be observed through his eyes. He was not going to be an utterly fearless man – that was implicit in his character already; besides, as he was going into danger he must recognize it as danger so that I, the writer, could record it as danger, subjectively and not editorially. We already know him to be a man of marked ability; he must also have the quality of leadership – that would develop out of his perceptiveness and sensitivity; it would be the kind of leadership that owes much to tact and little to animal spirits.

So, as the *Margaret Johnson* neared England, Hornblower's character was pretty well settled for him. The details had to be filled in. He would be a gangling and awkward man, because that would be an effective contrast with his mental ability, and would offer fuel for the fire of his self-criticism. But he would be an accomplished mathematician; I myself was constitutionally unable to make the leap from the binomial theorem to calculus, and it would be pleasant to have a hero to whom it was easy, especially as some of my close friends had been mathematicians. Yet, of course, in making Hornblower a mathematician I was indulging in shameless wish fulfilment, but it is only today, while writing these lines, that I realize it.

Besides being self-conscious he would be shy and reserved – those qualities are closely associated – so as to make his relationship with Lady Barbara more difficult, and there I would be able to help myself considerably; there was little I did not know about shyness and reserve from personal experience. And as regards his actual appearance, he obviously must have the indefinable good looks that a woman would notice and yet which he himself would under-estimate, and along with those good looks would go good hands, beautiful hands, perhaps; hands like that are often associated with the temperament I had in mind, and, once again, Hornblower would not be aware of their charm.

Another development. Lady Barbara's father, the first Lord Mornington, had been musical, and in fact had been a composer of minor distinction, while Wellington, her brother, had played the violin for his own pleasure until it interfered with his military studies. Lady Barbara would certainly be musical, too. Yet music had passed me by. I knew more – far more – about the etiquette of the court of Hapsburg–Lorraine than I did about harmony and counter-point. Something must be done to bar Lady Barbara and Hornblower from finding common ground in music, and for more reasons than one. The action

I eventually decided upon was perhaps drastic, even cold-blooded; Hornblower had to be tone-deaf, barred for ever from the pleasures of music. And that would help to keep him more human despite his intellectual eminence; a man I once knew well, and heartily disliked, had been tone-deaf, and had given me many opportunities of observing this condition. But if he had been a friend I suppose I should have profited in the same way from his infirmity.

One final point, before the *Margaret Johnson* sighted the Bishop Light and we entered the English Channel. This odd character had to have a name – so far he had been merely 'he' in my discussions with myself. He had to have a name which the reader would remember easily, which would stand out on the page, and which would not be confused with any other name. *War and Peace* had, in my judgment, almost not reached perfection because of the difficulty I had experienced in identifying the characters by their names. It would be desirable, but not entirely necessary for 'him' to have a slightly grotesque name – something more for his absurd self-consciousness to be disturbed about. The consideration of least weight – the merest milligram – was that 'he' was a slightly grotesque character, too. 'Horatio' came first to mind, and oddly enough not because of Nelson but because of Hamlet; but it met an essential requirement because it was a name with contemporary associations. Nelson was by no means the only Horatio in late Georgian times. Then, from Horatio, it seemed a natural and easy step to Hornblower. At one moment he was 'he'; at the next, 'Horatio'; and yet a moment later he was 'Captain Horatio Hornblower of His Britannic Majesty's Navy,' and the last awkward corner was turned and the novel practically ready to be written, and there was England fully in sight on the port bow.

16

THERE were things to be done before I could make a start. I had to get reacquainted with my wife and family; I had to re-adjust to the old environment; I had – most rebelliously – to deal with necessary business, and I had to do a great deal of reading to make sure of my facts. For once, in a way, there were so many obstacles to be surmounted that I even grew impatient. Instead of being driven, apprehensive and reluctant, into starting work, I was this time being held back from it, and with my natural cross-grainedness I chafed against the barriers. As always, there was the mounting curiosity regarding whether I could actually carry out the plans that were in my mind, especially as my reading progressed and the minor points were cleared up. The internal pressure reached a positively explosive point.

There was the constant slight irritation of having to explain myself, of having to make some sort of polite answer when asked, 'What's your subject this time?' That is a human enough question which I find extraordinarily hard to answer, even when I am actually writing, and practically impossible when I am not. There is one possible answer – 'Men and women' – but that can only be employed when rudeness has been amply justified. Why I should experience this difficulty is something I have never been able to explain to myself; there is some sort of mental cut-off system bringing about almost complete inhibition – something that functions nearly as efficiently as that which prevents a man from swallowing down his windpipe.

Michael Joseph was my publisher, and had been for years, and he had been my friend for years before that. He deserved an answer; I even *wanted* to answer him. For that matter there was the practical point that publishers have to plan their future production, and (I believe) prepare the ground for the books to come. So Joseph said, 'What next?' and I had to brace myself and splutter out a miserable answer. 'I'm thinking about writing a novel about a naval captain in 1808.' Joseph had read Henley, of course; he did not wince nor cry aloud. There was only a long pause and a blank stare before he answered, 'Splendid.' The magic of the year 1808 was imperceptible to him, and that was not his fault – to all except specialists, English naval history ended with Trafalgar, three years earlier. Even Joseph, as perceptive a man as I have ever known, could make no sense out of my tongue-tied efforts at explanation, not even when I added, 'I think I'll call him Hornblower,' and when we parted he was very little wiser and far more alarmed than before we met.

Nor could I blame him; the only person I could blame was myself, and I was nettled and irritated. It was only one more proof of the self-evident, of the fact that no book can be judged before it is written. So it came about that the very next morning I sat down at my table and pulled my pad toward me and wrote the words that had formulated themselves in my mind while I was drinking my breakfast coffee. 'It was not long after dawn that Captain Hornblower came up on the quarterdeck of the *Lydia*.' Perhaps it was a leap over the preliminary hurdle which I would not have taken in quite that fashion if I had not been goaded by that polite stare.

There followed the usual period of intense work, the inevitable fatigue, the loss of all sense of belonging to this world, which I had long ago come to expect and recognize, and then the thing was finished, sent off to the two publishers, and I could sink back into forgetfulness.

91

THE things that happened next make a puzzling sequence even to me. There is the matter of the lost novel, which I find almost inexplicable. The man I was then was different from the man I am now, and when I look back at myself there are numberless occasions when I find myself out of touch, experiencing the same hopeless feeling of addressing myself to a different kind of human being as fathers feel in discussions with their growing sons – for that matter I am old enough now to be a father to the man of those days, and I prefer not to think about what he would have thought of me if he had ever met me as I am now.

At any rate, there is this unsatisfactory matter of the lost novel, which demands a moment's attention at this point. Hornblower was finished, sent off, and forgotten. I cared so little about the book that when my American publishers suggested changing the title (American publishers always want to change titles) I agreed without thinking twice, so that the book was destined to be called *The Happy Return* in England and *Beat to Quarters* in America – a discrepancy which inconveniences me to this day. By the time the proofs came in I was deep in another novel – another set of waterlogged timbers had grown another crop of barnacles already; the fetid slime of my subconscious was seething with nutriment for low forms of life. And that novel was written, it was sent to London and to Boston, it was accepted, and was made the subject of signed agreements.

Then came the next development. There I was, recovering from my exertions, deep in a hundred activities all of them alien to literature, and enjoying ecstatically my hard-won freedom, when the old symptoms showed themselves again. They ran their course with feverish rapidity. Some time in 1809 or 1810, with the Peninsular War at its height, Bonaparte became concerned about the victualling of his garrison in Barcelona, which was in a state of semi-siege thanks to the activities of the Spanish *guerrilleros*. Land communications were difficult, and Bonaparte sent out a small squadron from Toulon under Admiral Cosmao with orders to break through to Barcelona carrying the necessary supplies. Cosmao met with the fate anyone could have predicted. His squadron was intercepted by a British naval force under Admiral Martin and destroyed. That was all, at first. That was the pioneer barnacle clinging to the timber.

Now came real life, horrible reality, unpleasant to remember and unpleasant to write about. General Franco had raised the standard of revolt in Spain, and the Spanish Civil War was tearing the country to pieces, and I was one of the men who went to try to find out what was happening. Fortunately

I do not have to go into details about what I saw; all that it is necessary for me to say here is that it was an extremely unhappy experience, during which there was never a moment to think about anything except what was going on around me. Everything was in stark and dreadful contrast with the trivial crises and counterfeit emotions of Hollywood, and I returned to England deeply moved and emotionally worn out.

The reservoirs refilled in time, and the old promptings reasserted themselves, and the inventive impulses made themselves felt once more. While in Spain I had, naturally, referred continually to what I knew of the Peninsular War; there were analogies and parallels, and there was the consistent Spanish national character to bear in mind. In the Peninsular War, command of the sea had been a vital factor; victory depended upon it even more than upon the admirable determination of the Spanish people never to submit to conquest. There was a possibility of a novel in this; when I started to come back to normal after my return I found that there had grown up in my mind a whole series of disconnected pictures of the feats the Royal Navy had performed during the war – the convoys destroyed, the signal stations blown up, the aid carried to the *guerrilleros*, the marching columns bombarded, the pin-prick raids upon the coast. Some sort of story – a story of considerable power, even – might be made of all this, with the underlying theme of the command of the sea.

And then – and then – here was the old surge of excitement, the intense realization that possibilities were expanding, were exploding. Who could best perform those feats? Who was the thinking and sensitive man who would be aware of the influence of sea power? Who but the discarded character in my last novel but one, Horatio Hornblower? The framework of history was exactly fitting; he would have made his 'happy return' just in time to be appointed to a ship of the line and to be sent out to operate on the Spanish coast, where (the Admiralty might well believe) his knowledge of the Spanish language would be useful. Hornblower was both mentally and technically equipped for coastal operations, with their need for expert ship handling and rapid extemporization of plans. And that attempt on the part of the French to revictual Barcelona; that would provide a climax for the story – Hornblower throwing himself between the French and their goal. Surely all this called for close consideration.

18

OF course it is foolish to be dogmatic regarding matters of taste, regarding artistic conventions, but it seems obvious that a novel (I am sure there are exceptions, but I cannot think of a single example) starts at one moment of rest and finishes at another. The moment of rest may be extremely fleeting, but it is indisputably there. If the action should already be under way in the opening paragraph it is necessary to go back in some later paragraph to explain how the action started. The action continues, it may transform itself into some further action, but sooner or later the action ceases even though there may be consequences and potentialities obvious to the reader when the novel ends. The conventional ending of a love story with a wedding is a hackneyed example.

Hornblower had come to life at the end of a period of rest with his entry into the Gulf of Fonseca; at his parting from Lady Barbara he had entered into another period of rest. Now we could find him leaving a period of rest – fitting out his new ship – and carry him through to another; that would be his final battle against the French squadron. And that final battle would have to be a glorious failure, in a sense. Somehow I did not feel it to be fitting for Hornblower to be too successful; it seemed better, more appropriate, that the novel should end with his naval career ruined, with him parted, until the end of the war at least, from his Maria, and his Barbara.

There were momentary bursts of pleasure at this point of the construction. There would be the opportunity, in fact the necessity, of bringing Maria to life; so far she had only been hinted at, and it would be necessary to construct a real person from those hints, as a paleontologist is supposed to be able to build up in his mind an entire dinosaur from a single bone. It was an interesting challenge, almost an amusing one. And Barbara; she would have to enter into the story. Only if it meant straining probability too far could she be omitted, so my judgment told me. I wanted her there as badly as Hornblower did. It could be managed, easily enough. Nothing could be more natural than that Barbara on her return to England should marry a distinguished admiral. Nothing could be more natural than that this admiral, with the influence of the Wellesleys behind him, should be given this new command-in-chief set up as a result of the Spanish revolt against the French. And surely it would be natural for Barbara to call her husband's attention to Hornblower's talents. She had seen those talents demonstrated; she must surely have a soft spot in her heart for him, whatever had happened between them. He was momentarily unemployed and here was this squadron being formed for action on the coast of Spain; everything seemed to fit. In my construction I had thought of the cart before I thought of the horse, but in the novel the horse would take his place in front of the cart naturally enough.

94

Such are the pleasures of construction; now, once again, with the jigsaw puzzle half completed and the picture becoming clear, it became increasingly easy to fit in the remaining pieces; all the odd barnacles that had grown up on the sunken timber were found to have their uses. A few more delirious days of half-conscious work and the whole story was ready, from start to finish. It only needed (here was a grim reminder of reality, the skeleton at the feast), it only needed to be written.

19

Now we must go back again to the lost novel – it almost deserves that name already because it has disappeared from this narrative after only the briefest mention some pages back. The typescripts were lying in Boston and London, and soon they would be going to the printers. And I did not want that novel to appear yet, not if I were going to write *Ship of the Line*. It would not be fitting for it to be published between these two books. There was something inartistic (hateful though that word might be) about such a scheme. *Ship of the Line* was demanding to be written. There was one obvious course to take, and that was to postpone publication of the lost novel.

I wish I could remember more about that novel. It was contemporary, and it contained at least one murder and a hint of incest, and the principal characters (I think) were women, but I cannot recover any additional details. Every three or four years something reminds me of it, and then I forget about it again. Cynically, I suspect that it was a bad novel, which makes me content to continue in ignorance; presumably I was in my usual state of disappointment over finished work, but I do not believe that influenced me – consciously. However it was, London and Boston were informed that I had changed my mind about publication, that to fill the gap I was going to write a sequel to *The Happy Return*, and that I would have this ready for publication at the time originally planned for the publication of the discarded novel.

Looking back, I am astounded at the light-heartedness of all this. My publishers took it more seriously than I did; I distinctly remember the arrival of a long and solemn telegram from Boston in which the pros and cons were carefully debated, but it arrived after I had started the actual writing of *Ship of the Line* and I was no longer in a fit state to view mere practical matters with any balance at all. I was off in another world; and, as always at the moment of starting, this book would be far better than any predecessor, and who cared what happened to some other miserable novel already half forgotten? So the lost novel was really lost. It is just possible that the typescripts still exist, that they lie forgotten and gathering dust, in rarely entered storerooms in Boston and Bloomsbury; some day someone may find himself in one of those storerooms and wonder vaguely what is this wad of typescript he has stumbled over. I am perfectly content to let the matter remain like that. My literary executors can debate the ethics of publication.

20

So *Ship of the Line* was written, tumultuously, with a genuine reason for haste besides the invariable and inadequate one of my own impatience. The title was fixed from the start, but most of my titles are; knowing what will be the title of the book while it is being written is closely allied to knowing what the end of the book will be; it stands beside the goal faintly perceived in the mind's eye, as the writing makes its weary way towards the end. The ship herself, Hornblower's command, H.M.S. *Sutherland*, somehow won my special affection. Her Dutch build – like most of her contemporaries, she had entered the Royal Navy as a prize – was of considerable service to Hornblower and to me, and she was something of an ugly duckling of whom I grew fond.

There was a ridiculous incident just when I had begun the first chapter. I was dining in some Armenian restaurant or other – fatigue had not yet asserted itself to the extent of making all food indifferent to me – and had ordered the almost inevitable shish kebab. Here it came; pieces of bell pepper, pieces of lamb, pieces of mushroom, pieces of onion, a score or more items on a skewer. A firm grip on the skewer, a long push with a fork, and there it all lay in a tumbled heap on my plate. An analogy shot into my mind as I sat and stared at it. This book I was beginning to write (which I could not help being conscious of, whatever the business of the moment) was going to be something like this. Cutting out expeditions, convoy battles, shore raids would be the peppers and onion and bits of lamb. And the skewer which held them together and gave them form or reason? That would be H.M.S. *Sutherland* under the command of her renowned captain. I think that must have been the moment when my affection for that ship started to sprout; I know that from that time on I had to use restraint in my writing lest sentiment should creep in. And to this day, more than twenty-five years later, the sight of shish kebab on a skewer calls up to my mind's eye a three-dimensional picture of a blue sea and a hot sun and H.M.S. *Sutherland* standing in under easy sail to her rendezvous off Palamós Point. Sentiment, shish kebab, and *Sutherland;* an odd trio inextricably associated.

Hornblower and his *Sutherland* started from their moment of rest and went

96

on to their moment of rest; the book was finished and the typescripts sent off comfortably in time for the promised day of publication, one year exactly after *The Happy Return*. It had been a full year and there was the usual numb bewilderment at the easing of the demand for mental activity. With the return of sensation, second thoughts began to creep in. The details of my day-to-day life at that time are naturally (perhaps mercifully) blurred in my memory; the only thing I can be sure of is that I was active (as always) domestically and socially; reading omnivorously; travelling and even writing (at that time I was under contract to deliver a weekly column to a newspaper); making up feverishly for the three months which had dropped out of my life on account of *Ship of the Line*.

21

THE second thoughts crept in insidiously. One of my bedside books (it is my habit to read dry factual books – even the *Encyclopaedia Britannica* – before going to sleep) was a volume of unedited letters of Napoleon I, letters which for obvious reasons had not appeared in the official collection issued by Napoleon III. Here was a letter to his brother Joseph, the intrusive King of Spain. 'The five or six persons who have been arrested at Bilbao by General Merlin, must be put to death.' Nearly all these letters revealed Bonaparte as utterly unscrupulous, and as utterly merciless when he thought his interests, his precious prestige, were imperilled. There could be found hints of his desire for vengeance – even though vengeance might be impolitic –perhaps traceable to his Corsican boyhood. And Hornblower was at this moment a prisoner in Bonaparte's hands – Hornblower, who had struck such shrewd blows at his dominion over Spain, who had fooled his generals and who had the audacity, the insolence, to violate the sacred soil of France. There were detestable examples in plenty of Bonaparte's mean indulgence in personal revenge. Alvarez of Gerona, Hofer of the Tyrol, had been done to death when generosity would have cost him nothing. Bonaparte must have hated the very name of Hornblower, and – on one occasion, on the coast of Spain, Hornblower had sailed under false colours, under the French flag.

This was a legitimate ruse of war; there were frequent examples in history, one notable one during the opening moves of the attack on Quebec in 1759. But to Bonaparte it might well supply an excuse for indulgence in his thirst for revenge, while he had in his power one of the very few English captains ever to be taken prisoner during the Napoleonic Wars. To have Hornblower shot would gratify Bonaparte's desire for revenge; to charge an English captain with a gross violation of the laws of war might help to explain to France and Europe why the Imperial Navy had not been over-successful lately. But perhaps something less than actual murder might satisfy Bonaparte, or at least might be deemed by him to be more profitable. To try Hornblower and condemn him, scare him nearly to death, and then pardon him with a great show of generosity, would be (in Bonaparte's judgment) an effective piece of theatre, like the celebrated incident of the burning of the letter in the presence of the Countess von Hatzfeldt. Perhaps Lady Barbara could make a personal appeal to Bonaparte on Hornblower's behalf? No. That was not quite right; or perhaps it was a theme not susceptible to sufficient elaboration. I was following a false scent.

That was a surprise to me; it seemed an admission that there was a scent to follow, and here I was in bed trying to go to sleep, and I knew from long experience that there was no surer way of inhibiting sleep than to dally with plots at midnight. Besides, I had left Hornblower a prisoner of war; the novel was about to be published, and I wanted nothing more to do with him. So I put down the *Lettres Inédites* and turned out my bedside light and composed myself to sleep, and an hour later I was out of bed seeking a drearier book still which might bring me some distraction from these nagging thoughts.

22

Of course the plot formed itself; if it would not show on the surface, it burrowed below it like a mole. If Hornblower was not to be formally pardoned, he would have to escape from captivity – there was a fairly extensive literature dealing with escape from Imperial prisons, but nothing I had read was either satisfactory or suggestive. Besides, by 1810 so much of Europe was under French domination that it would be impossible, were he to escape, for him to reach a neutral country. He would have to reach the sea. Of course he would have to reach the sea; there could be no compromise about that. I found myself actually yearning for it to come about; I wanted quite passionately for Hornblower to escape from the confinement that, with his temperament, he would find so insupportable, to escape from the treacherous land to the freedom of the sea. It would be a long and tricky journey.

Now came one of those sudden moments when one idea unexpectedly adheres to another apparently quite alien. I made the discovery at the usual neutral moment when I was glancing through the morning's letters, even though not one of those letters related to the business of Hornblower's escape. Some years before I had taken a motorboat down the river Loire; I put down an unread letter to face a new realization that Hornblower could use the same route to the sea. A small boat – and I had spent months, perhaps a total of years in small boats – on a river was a very convenient means of transport for a fugitive. It eliminated the possibility of losing one's way, it offered a convenient method of carrying necessary stores and equipment, and it would help considerably towards evading those inspections of passports and demands for papers to which travellers by road were continually subjected in Imperial France. Particularly would this be the case on the Loire, which I knew from personal experience to be lonely, unfrequented, apparently unnavigable, and yet practicable.

The blood was stirring in my veins; at the limit of deep sea navigation on the Loire was the city of Nantes. Seagoing vessels came up as far as the quays there – I could remember them. Perhaps Hornblower could – a sudden boiling over, and when the flurry had died down the mental picture was formed, of Hornblower recapturing the *Witch of Endor;* it was vivid and urgent in my mind. There were logical and interlocking corollaries, too. To perform such a feat Hornblower would need assistance, and skilled assistance. He would have to have Bush and Brown with him. That meant they would have to be with him on his journey down the Loire, and that called up further mental pictures; Hornblower in command of a ship's company of three; a twenty-foot boat instead of a two-thousand-ton seventy-four – there was a sort of wry and yet dramatic quality about that situation which demanded, insisted upon, consideration. Something was certainly happening to my prejudice against dealing with Hornblower again.

23

SOMETHING else happened. The proofs of *Ship of the Line* arrived, and I had set myself to read them, with all my usual reluctance. Then my small, but elder, son looked over my shoulder to see what I was doing. 'Oh, hurry up and finish that, Daddy,' he said. 'I want to read it. I liked the first one so much.' That son now has a son himself of just that age, but the gratification I felt at that moment is still fresh in my memory. It was compensation – overpayment – not merely for the trials of parenthood but for the labours of writing. And, sentiment apart (why was sentiment so distrusted by the man who was me at that time?) the incident inevitably helped to reconcile me to the notion of writing another novel about Hornblower.

Michael Joseph helped to stir the witches' brew. I was trying to explain to him about the turmoil that I was feeling, and I was struggling with my life-long prejudice against ever putting into words to a single soul, the half-

99

formed ideas that were engrossing me. But somehow I was able to convey to him the tenuous theme I had in mind. 'You want to bring him back with flying colours?' said Joseph. This time it was his turn to be met with a blank stare, as if the remark had not raised a ripple. Nor could it; it had fallen, not into the liquid and lively river of polite conversation, but into the sluggish slime of the subconscious, sinking down and farther down to stimulate the barnacles into increased reproduction.

The effect was naturally contrariwise. Plain triumph, unadulterated success, was not the theme I was seeking. For that matter I had myself enjoyed considerable personal success, and I was acutely aware that 'enjoy' was by no means the correct word to use. The cross-grainedness of human nature meant that the gift horse had always to be looked in the mouth, and found to be long in the tooth; some rose leaf always to be found crumpled, while simple fate, and extraneous events, were bound to add bitter to the sweet, rough to the smooth, in addition to mixing the metaphors. It would serve Hornblower right if the same thing happened to him; but also (let us at all costs keep sentiment out of literature) there was the certainty that this would be artistically (that hateful word again) satisfactory.

The days went by, and the other ideas which had been growing in my mind began to join on – ideas at first apparently unrelated, even regarded at first as the germs of some different piece of work. I had been observing the development of a theme of a thwarted, transient love affair; hot passion gratified and yet cut short. Of course, it must have been Hornblower that it happened to. Why had it not occurred to me before? Hornblower making love, if not with one eye on the clock, then with his mind full of rival thoughts. Hornblower, as always, lucky and yet discontented, quite incapable of self-abandon; Hornblower, the sort of man with whom any woman might fall deeply in love, and yet whom a discerning or intuitive woman would recognize as one neither to hold nor to bind. It was bound to happen to him sooner or later, when he had a little leisure. And in France at this moment the *réfractaires* were beginning to make themselves felt, the young men who were on the run to avoid conscription; there had been a momentary consideration of the possibility that Hornblower might find help from some of them in his escape – and in France there had been also a growing body of more mature public opinion opposed to Bonaparte because of liberal convictions, or simply from contemplation of the disastrous results of Bonapartism. Half a dozen pieces of the jigsaw fell into position now. I knew where Hornblower would find the necessary help and how he would have his love affair.

There were some final decisions to be made. There was a death sentence to be passed – two, in fact. Poor Mrs Hornblower. Her death was decreed, not without hesitation, not without unavailing compassion; I seemed to know her so well. But there was no place left for her, and her death would be a very bitter ingredient in the cup of Hornblower's success. It would not be a difficult matter to arrange, for she was already pregnant in the last novel, and death in childbirth was common enough in those days to escape comment. She had been made pregnant to enable me to score a particular point in *Ship of the Line*, and now the fact was additionally useful, almost as if I had had the next development in mind at the time. I can affirm quite truthfully that this was not the case, but I suppose it is just possible that somewhere down among the barnacles, quite unrecognized, her approaching death had been planned. As for the death of Admiral Leighton – Barbara's husband – there would be no difficulty about that. He was a sailor in active service, and it was quite certain that he would be soon fighting his way into Rosas Bay to destroy the ships Hornblower had disabled there. I could be quite sure that few would shed a tear over Leighton's fate – perhaps not even Barbara.

24

So now it began to look as if the novel were ready for the writing. Certainly the old restlessness began to assert itself. There was the same lure, the temptation to discover if I could really fix on paper the complexities and moods that were circulating in my mind. There was the same quite unreasoning hope that this novel would be easier to write than the last. There was the same taking of the plunge. The day came when I wrote 'Page 1' and 'Chapter I,' and Admiral Leighton launched his attack on Rosas Bay. The work went along well enough, if 'well enough' can be construed as including the inevitable daily exhaustion. Colonel Caillard and his gendarmes arrived to carry off Hornblower and Bush and Brown, just after Hornblower had learned enough about Leighton's fate to leave him in distressing uncertainty for the next few months. Everything was normal, until the shock came, almost as sudden and every bit as painful as walking into the edge of a door in the dark. One morning, while planning my day's work, I was filled with horrible doubts, and blindly ignored them; the next day those doubts were certainties and I was faced with disaster.

I cannot explain how it had come about, how I had been so incredibly careless, so blind, so inattentive. At this point in my construction of the story I had blandly said to myself 'here they escape,' and had actually thought no more about it. I had left a gap and I had done nothing to fill it. By some unprecedented lapse I had not even realized that a gap existed until I found it yawning at my feet. They had to escape; they had to escape from an escort of twenty gendarmes in the heart of France, and Bush was only beginning to recover from the amputation of his foot – he could not walk a yard. How in the world could they possibly escape? There could be no question of leaving Bush behind – Hornblower would never have done such a thing, and in any case Bush would be badly needed in the remainder of the story. I had loaded myself with difficulties; I had made *l'affaire Hornblower* so important that in addition to the escort I had put one of Bonaparte's ablest police officers in charge; Colonel Caillard would leave no opportunity for escape that I could avail myself of.

For me this was a moment of disruption. I was ashamed of myself, shocked at my behaviour, consumed with doubts as to my fitness for my chosen profession. But that was only the long view; the immediate and pressing future was momentarily more important.

The story had come to a complete stop, and there seemed to be no way out of the impasse into which I had hastened so blindly. I might have to back out and take another route altogether. But that meant recasting the whole story, beginning the construction anew, and, after reconstruction, rewriting; and it was fifteen years since I had rewritten one single chapter. So far in this book I had written five chapters. Must I rewrite them all? As usual my passionate and unreasoning prejudices against having anything to do with finished work were stirred up until I was in a state of panic. But how could a man with one foot newly amputated escape from twenty gendarmes?

Of course he escaped in the end. I was to find that my profession has its privileges as well as its burdens, and luck was on my side. Two days (I think) of the most anxious thought and I worked out the solution – two days of pacing up and down my workroom each morning, and of walking frantically through unsympathetic streets each afternoon and night. Not for nothing had Hornblower acquired the habit of pacing his quarterdeck when he had a problem to solve. I expect those two days were filled with moments when my children shrank from me in terror; I cannot believe that physical weariness would blunt my anxiety.

But the writer has the powers with which witches and warlocks were once credited. He can summon up storms and floods. Fortunately the weather was on my side in any case; *Sutherland*'s battle had taken place in late autumn and now it was winter, and a snowstorm was not only possible but actually likely. A snowstorm – a river – a boat – a flood – and my three characters had escaped, as anyone who troubles to read Chapter Six may see. And I had been through such an experience that I would never be the same again, or so I thought. Indeed, for a few days after that incident I would have grudgingly admitted (if I had ever discussed the subject) that there were worse things than the day-to-day writing of a novel, just as a man who has once tasted the strappado might admit there were worse things than the rack.

25

NOT so many days later there was another new experience, as clear in my memory even now as the one just recounted. Hornblower was on the move again; his love affair with Marie de Graçay was over – or at least in abeyance – and he was making the descent of the Loire with his two companions. There was trouble ahead of him, and trouble behind, but at that moment he was as free from trouble as he could ever hope to be. I know that feeling so well myself; I found myself envying Hornblower while simultaneously feeling in deep accord with him. Hornblower was happier at this time than a life of action and hardship had ever allowed him to be so far. He was still the Man Alone, but he was experiencing the comradeship and personal intimacy which – partly through his own faults of personality – had so far evaded him. He was experiencing the pleasures of the land, seeing beauty all new to him, like the dawn creeping mistily over a silent river, or a line of willows against the background of the different green of the hills. He was on the move, too – a necessity for the happiness of a restless fellow like him – but sedately, without pressure, and with a sufficiency of trivial incidents (such as finding a channel through sandbanks) to keep his active mind from racketing itself into discontent.

There were one or two mornings while I was writing these passages when I actually observed, with considerable astonishment – perhaps even dismay – that I was going eagerly to my worktable, that I was looking forward to a morning with Hornblower while he was, for once, in a way, in a tranquil state of mind. There was a momentary temptation to prolong the voyage; certainly there was a faint regret that the Loire was not as long as the Amazon. But geography as well as history opposed any self-indulgence. So did something still more important; the necessity for keeping a balance, for obeying the dictates of my artistic judgment, my literary taste. (Those hateful words again, always seeking to creep in like disease bacteria into the human body.) The story demanded a certain modicum of happiness, but to increase it beyond a particular point would destroy the equilibrium. My taste and judgment told me that there should be so much, and no more. In a rather similar mood to

Gibbon's, I sighed as a sentimentalist and obeyed as a craftsman; I found wry consolation in thinking of some *chef de cuisine* setting himself to compose a master dish, and exercising the necessary restraint regarding the herbs he personally favoured. So Hornblower went on to Nantes, to honour and distinction, and the wave of publicity which he found so distasteful.

26

Six years went by before he came back into my life again, to find me a changed man, physically at least. I have written about this experience briefly before, and so I approach this writing with my usual distaste for finished work. I was now an invalid, or I was told I was one, or I thought I was one. One of the symptoms of old age had made its appearance, somewhat prematurely, twenty years or so before it might be expected. My arteries were closing up – please forgive these anatomical details – and the assumption was that the process would continue. I found myself limited in my walking, in my ability to climb stairs, and my distances diminished with the weeks, so that soon I could not walk more than fifty yards, or climb more than a single flight of stairs, without pain enough to make further effort impossible without rest. And the future was gloomy; soon my extremities would be starved of blood, and then would follow amputation and helplessness.

There was no comfort in the future at all. I could not guess – neither could the doctors – that I was a freak, a unique case, about whom articles (pleasingly impersonal) would be written in the technical press, that the disease was going to halt itself (in a way never before known) on the very brink of total disaster. The doctors were grimly advising me to find a house without stairs so that I could be wheeled about, and they said, also, that a life of complete inactivity, of doing nothing, of avoiding every kind of excitement and exertion (even mental) might postpone the worst for a brief while.

Naturally, I tried it, and inevitably I found it impossible. To sit in gloom and await dissolution is not a practice to be recommended to anybody. Moreover, there were the bomb ketches. I have to acknowledge – ridiculous though it may sound – a great personal debt to bomb ketches. In my recreational reading bomb ketches had shown up repeatedly – the curious and highly specialized craft that had been devised for the purpose of throwing shells from the sea at targets on land, especially (by virtue of the lofty trajectory of their mortars) targets in dead ground behind hills or fortifications. They were employed in frequent amphibious operations during the Napoleonic Wars, and in peacetime they often found a use in Arctic exploration, because their sturdy construction enabled them to withstand the stresses of the ice. Nelson himself had once made an Arctic voyage in a bomb ketch.

It would be interesting to work out some hypothetical campaign in which bomb ketches played an important role. Of course that would involve the employment of a whole squadron – the bomb vessels always needed cover from attack by more powerful ships of war. They had been employed repeatedly against Bonaparte's invasion fleet in the Channel ports, but without great success, even under Nelson's command. They were a weapon of surprise and opportunity, and even Bonaparte's admirals knew about the potentialities of bomb vessels, and could take elementary precautions against them.

Surprise and opportunity! Something was happening to me, something I thought was never going to happen again – and something which, according to the doctors, should not be allowed to happen. Here were the stirrings of invention, that pleasant feeling of recognition, like the pricking of the witch's thumbs. And here, too, was an enormous wave of relief that these symptoms were appearing, something normal in a grossly abnormal world. Those blessed words, surprise and opportunity, could be allowed to sink down into my subconscious and stir up things there. And if they brought amputation any nearer I was in the mood to say it was worth it.

Bomb ketches; they had been employed in the second British attack on Copenhagen in 1807; Wellington had seen action there as a divisional general. But that was a formal battle with due warning given – no room for surprise and not much opportunity. And Wellington had a brother-in-law, although he was to live another fifty years and never know he even had a sister.

So now the gloomy mornings were no longer gloomy; they were enlivened by the entrancing discoveries of what had happened during the night without my volition. Additions came hurrying in, especially now that Hornblower had made his reappearance into the debate, although without formal recognition. He was barred from consideration, yet remembering him caused a twinge of regret, for I realized that I had finished with him on the threshold of an interesting period in his career, married at last to his Barbara, whom he respected and whom he would come as near to loving as his limited capacity would ever allow. Hornblower learning to be a country squire would make an interesting picture. On the other hand, following his public and personal triumph, he was bound to be given some important employment, for the Napoleonic Wars were by no means over. The Admiralty might find difficulty in discovering the right hole in which to put such a square peg as Hornblower, all the same. He was no more than halfway up the captains' list. Hornblower commanding a ship of the line, one of twenty or so enduring the endless monotony of the blockade service, might make an interesting psychological study. But as Hornblower was finished as far as I was concerned there was no satisfaction – rather the reverse – in these speculations about his later career. Much better to return to our bomb ketches.

Of course, there was the Baltic. That was where the next vital developments in the world-wide war were going to take place. That was where bomb ketches could be employed – shallow waters, and important coastal trade, while repeated and rapid changes of national policy might offer the necessary surprises and opportunities. There was the burning question as to whether Bonaparte would actually go to war with Alexander of Russia. British diplomacy had worked hard to maintain Alexander in his obstinate attitude towards the French Empire; and where British diplomacy was at work the Royal Navy was not far behind.

Of course! Of course! (The really gratifying moments of construction are always introduced by 'of course' instead of by 'perhaps'). Bonaparte was trying to enforce his Continental System along every mile of coast, and, while he was planning his surprise attack on Russia, and eventually when he launched his left wing in an advance on St Petersburg, he had an immensely long and very vulnerable line of communications along the southern shore of the Baltic. That was the ideal scene of operations for bomb ketches. I knew a British squadron in actual fact had pushed its way up into the Baltic. There was need for an active and ingenious naval officer there, not afraid of responsibility, capable of understanding a diplomatic problem, capable of stiffening the moody and incalculable Alexander, capable of threading his way through the convolutions of neutrality laws – and with bomb ketches under his command ready for instant employment. And, of course, that officer would be Hornblower.

He was of just sufficient seniority for it to be quite reasonable for him to be appointed commodore of a small squadron – say a ship of the line, a couple of sloops, a couple of bomb ketches – and entrusted with the immense responsibility which, however much he might worry about it, sweetened the air he breathed. Of course it would be Hornblower. The fragments joined up as if endowed with minds of their own. Spring, and the opening of navigation in the Baltic, would come just when Hornblower had had long enough leave, after his last adventures, to discover what it was like to be a country squire and the husband of Lady Barbara. There was the curious and involved question of the neutrality of Swedish Pomerania – and the behaviour of the

French troops who eventually overran the province constituted a classic example of what happens when soldiers unpaid and unfed break loose from the control of generals devoid of feelings. There was Sweden, now under the rule of a Marshal of the Empire.

And (of course!) the left-hand prong of Bonaparte's attack on Russia, directed against St Petersburg while he himself marched on Moscow, had been held up at Riga – there had been a desperate amphibious, and unsuccessful, siege, and the subsequent retreat of the French had been marked by the defection of the Prussian contingent, which presaged the disintegration of the Empire. If Hornblower needed troubled waters in which to go a-fishing he could ask for nothing more troubled than the Baltic in 1812; there he would carry as much responsibility as any man could desire. At Riga he could use his precious bomb ketches, and, for once, justice could be done him by allowing him to be actually present at the moment when the French Empire reached its farthest point of conquest. Lastly (had we come as far as 'lastly'?) if Hornblower were not safely employed up the Baltic there was the danger (which I did not like to contemplate) that it would be his bombs that burst in the air over Baltimore.

So the decision had been reached without my even knowing that a decision lay ahead. It only remained to complete the work of construction, to perform all the pleasant, logical tasks of deciding on a beginning and an end, settling the sequence of events within the framework of history and geography – it was fifteen years since I had last breathed the keen air of the Baltic, but my memory fortunately still served – to invent and then to select, to exercise my judgment and taste; all this was so completely different from the miserable attempt to live the life of a cabbage in grim resignation that, really, only the hackneyed metaphor of the change from hell to heaven could adequately describe the difference.

27

THERE was at least one important change in technique. I was quite surprised to find out how much thinking I had always done before on my feet. When a special piece of construction had been called for in the old days – when, for instance, it was necessary to provide adequate means for some expression of Hornblower's feelings, or, more desperately, to invent the circumstances in which he could escape from Colonel Caillard, it had been second nature to walk about so as to set the mechanism of thought to work. It was while I was walking, sometimes deliberately for that purpose, sometimes merely because I was walking to arrive somewhere where I needed to be, that ideas generated themselves, and not merely these lesser ideas, but sometimes whole major pieces of invention.

Now walking was impossible; I had to find other ways of allowing my mind to act. The habit of thinking while walking had begun in boyhood and had established itself during a creative life of more than twenty years. I could no more deliberately think out a new system than I could deliberately invent a new plot; the substitutes came by fortunate accident. There were the little mathematical puzzles; nothing very advanced, almost pure arithmetic, exercises in logic rather than in algebra, which I used to invent and then set myself to solve. It called for some small ingenuity and considerable patience to prove, beyond dispute, that A could only be seven and X could only be nine in the example I had before me. And in the little intervals of thinking about the puzzle I could think about the plot; arithmetic carried construction along with it as a sponge carries water.

And the absurd, ridiculous game I devised related to the drinking of soup. I have never spoken about this to a soul; this is a first and public confession. Dinner begins, and a bowl of soup is put before me. Then I must estimate the amount of soup in the bowl, and the capacity of the spoon, and calculate how many spoonfuls it will take to finish the soup – all this, of course, while carrying on the polite chatter that goes with soup. Then the spoonfuls must be counted, one by one, while maintaining at least the outward appearance of a sane and normal person. Dr Johnson on a stroll could keep count of the beats of his walking-stick and still go on talking; I can do the same with spoonfuls of soup, even during the mounting excitement resulting from reaching the twenty-fourth spoonful and observing that only about three more remain when my original estimate was of a total of twenty-eight. Why that should help Hornblower devise a means of bringing his bomb ketches within range of the French siege batteries I cannot imagine, but luckily it did.

28

So construction was completed and the book was ready to be written, and the eternal question as to when, or whether, to start, presented itself in aggravated form. I had been warned under dire penalties never to incur fatigue, to do nothing that might cause a rise in blood pressure, and I knew only too well how laborious was the process of composition, of visualization. I told myself that a sensible man would be content with all the pleasure of construction and would now go back to the life of a cabbage and carry with him to the grave the secrets of Hornblower's campaign in the Baltic.

That was just the point. Putting it into those words made it instantly and abundantly clear that I could not bear to do anything of the sort. The thing simply had to be written. I had to face the unsavoury fact that I was an exhibitionist at least. Until that moment the logical sequences of construction, composition and publication had gone unanalyzed. It had never occurred to me that those sequences were by no means fixed and immutable, but could perhaps be broken off by a mere exercise of will. I think I had even told myself, on occasions, that a piece of work could not be considered completed until it was in print and presented to the public; now I realized that I was only finding an excuse, that really I urgently wanted to publish my work, to exhibit it. However much, and however genuinely, I disliked personal appearances; however much I disliked meeting strangers, I yet wanted to do so vicariously. I make my fleeting personal entrances into the literary world with almost the same reluctance with which I would take my clothes off in Trafalgar Square, but there was a decided and definite pleasure – more than that, a positive need – in regard to pushing Hornblower out into the world.

This admission introduced a new factor into the situation; bluntly, the fear of death. I had to contemplate the possibility that I might die before the *Commodore* was finished, and – especially from the point of view of the Commodore – I disliked the idea intensely. It was not so much that I would be sorry if the world were to miss a masterpiece, but rather that the masterpiece would miss the world. To leave it unfinished would be perhaps even worse than leaving it unwritten altogether – all the old discussion about Edwin Drood used to irritate me profoundly. Hornblower had attracted sufficient attention by now for it not to be a wild impossibility for an unfinished *Commodore* to call up some considerable speculation as to how he would have been finished, and the thought of someone else trying it, the thought of the silly things that might be said, drove me into a panic. There were now most pressing reasons to begin the writing, and even more pressing reasons to complete it. But while the writing was going on there were also definite reasons for moderation; I felt in exactly the same situation as if I were driving a car low on gas in an effort to reach a filling station – to drive too fast would simply defeat my own object, however great the temptation. There was a certain optimum speed that would have to be maintained, and, luckily, with a long experience behind me, I knew all about that optimum speed; it was what I had always tried to maintain while writing some twenty-odd books previously, when the matter was not of such desperate importance.

There was a mingling of regret and satisfaction when I contemplated the fact that there were no written notes for some literary executor to look through. I had never made written notes in my life; it had always been too much trouble, and I was certainly not going to start now. Moreover, I was quite sure that written notes – like conversations with a publisher across a luncheon table – could not convey anything like the impression I wanted to make, and I am equally sure of that to this day. Only on the evidence of the finished book could the book be judged.

So there was my mind made up for me. I sat myself at my work-table and sat Sir Horatio down in his hip bath, ready to go to take command of the precious bomb ketches which had triggered all this off, and the work of composition began. It ran its usual course, hardly different from its predecessors. A change of method was necessary in the writing as in the construction. I discovered – what I had never realized before – that it was my habit to get up from my work-table and pace the room at quite frequent intervals. Partly, this was to ease my stiff joints, partly to allow my mind to debate some minor point. Would it be better if someone's mood were to be expressed editorially, or revealed by his speeches? Should the text of a written order be given, or should it be summarized? I was surprised to find how often I took a turn around the room in order to settle these questions of taste. Yet walking was a hundred times more tiring than it used to be – at the end of two hours' work I would now have walked the equivalent of fifty miles to a fit person. It could not be done, and it did not take more than a day or two's experimenting to prove it to me. Luckily, supremely fortunately, trial and error (mostly unconscious) supplied a solution. Now I stand up, as the result of the habit of years, and then have to decide whether the point is serious enough to justify walking, and that in itself will clear up the difficulty as often as not. Otherwise I stand erect and gaze into space long enough to loosen the sitting-joints, until the already written work lying before me attracts my attention so that I sit down again and glance through the earlier paragraphs. The mere act of doing so will carry me over the momentary difficulty, like a horse who has refused a fence but who will make the leap at the second attempt if he is allowed a good look at the obstacle and then given a fair run at it.

29

THE book was finished. During the hours of visualization I had been living in a world in which arteriosclerosis played no part; during the other hours of the day there had been, first, the usual numbness when the personal troubles lost their edge; to be succeeded by the irrepressible interest in the approaching day's work. Three months had gone by, and I still lived – more important, the accursed disease had made no progress – and I had learned that it was perfectly possible to face the rest of life as a handicapped person. Hornblower had brought inexpressible benefits. In later years I was able to estimate the magnitude of those benefits by re-reading the book, disregarding the inevitable distaste with which I approach past work. There it is, a book of adventure, sometimes of tension, an analysis of action and responsibility. Its literary merits do not enter into this discussion (I will not say fortunately), but the interesting conclusion is that it is not an unhappy book; I really do not believe that anyone could guess that it was written by a man going through a period of profound gloom – I must add here that at that time I was experiencing all sorts of other violent personal troubles which I shall not mention further. The fact that no hint of them is apparent in its pages is the clearest proof of the intensity of feeling occasioned by the act of writing, and, as I have already said, it is also a proof of the debt I owe to that book.

One small incidental point; the *Commodore* appeared as a serial in the *Saturday Evening Post*, to which I had become a frequent contributor. This was always with the feeling that my work was not quite suited to such a medium – not quite that I was a fish out of water there, but more as if I had strayed by accident into some strange house filled with unfamiliar furnishings. And in the *Commodore* there was a certain small amount of adultery. Not even very profound adultery, if such an adjective is permissible. But it was adultery, all the same, and never before, not since the days of Benjamin Franklin, had adultery made any appearance at all in the pages of the *Saturday Evening Post*. It really caused quite a flutter. Many American newspapers commented on the fact; so did innumerable readers. It was the first rift in the dike of convention, and there was no little boy handy to put his finger into the hole. Before very long topics that had been barred for a century and a half were being freely discussed in the pages of the *Post*. The commodore was not the cause of all this, but he certainly was the *Saturday Evening Post's* first adulterer.

There was an odd reason for that adultery, too – I suppose there is an odd reason for most adulteries, but this one I consider odder than most. Hornblower was destined at the end of the book to come down with typhus, the jail-fever that killed off whole armies that winter, and typhus is a disease transmitted by lice. I knew – more than one volume of memoirs mention the fact – that dignitaries of the Russian court were usually carriers of body vermin, and I wanted to show Hornblower with at least a flea, and he had to be provided with ample opportunity for acquiring a minimum of one. He also, like many mercurial souls, did not carry his liquor well; and the bond that united him to his Barbara was as frail as any bond would prove to be when applied to Hornblower; so that one way and another that adultery was pretty inevitable. But I fancy that Hornblower picked up the louse that gave him typhus at some moment when he was helping to defend the village of Daugavgriva, that place whose name might well have become historic if it had not been so unpronounceable.

<h2 style="text-align:center">30</h2>

By the time the *Commodore* was finished the world was a happier place for me, and, incidentally, the clouds were lifting all over the world with the victories of the Allies over Germany and Japan. I had discovered that it was perfectly possible to live a full life without ever walking more than fifty yards at a time – and I will take this opportunity of saying once and for all that for twenty years I have lived under that handicap and have never ceased to enjoy myself. But, equally important, the disease had somehow halted, despite the fact that I had done some heavy work. Optimism was beginning to creep in, and I could return to life.

The first piece of work I was given to do under these new conditions was commissioned – naturally – by the Allied governments, and the terms of reference were, in themselves, highly optimistic along certain lines. Mr Churchill and Mr Roosevelt were quite certain that the Hitler government and the defences of Germany were about to collapse. That collapse seemed imminent to anyone reading the newspapers, but it was reassuring to be told that the highest authorities thought so too. But those same authorities also expected that Japan would put up a long and desperate defence even after the fall of Germany. It was something I did not clearly understand, for my geography lessons at school had emphasized that Japan, like England, was an island power which would be forced into rapid surrender on losing command of the sea, but the authorities believed differently now, and said so. Of course it was only one half of the authorities' mind that believed this – the other half knew about the progress of the atomic bomb without a great deal of confidence in its efficacy.

What Washington and London feared was that the public both in England and America, over-confident with the fall of Germany, would be set back by the prospect of a long and bloody campaign in the Pacific, and would insist on a premature, unsatisfactory peace. So my task was to prepare public opinion for this next development, and to set about it even while the Allied armies were poised along the Rhine, gathering strength for the final blow. As a result I was established in Washington with a free run through the departments of the Department of the Navy, having all the secrets revealed to me as to the difficulties of delivering a massive attack against Japan across the vast distances of the Pacific. There was the magic word 'logistics,' which I heard on every side. In dazed fashion I read through vast lists of the necessary shipping and specialized equipment that would be called for. I listened to serious – desperately serious – debates as to what would be the reaction of the United States Army when it would be summoned fresh from the conquest of Germany, to undertake the even more difficult conquest of Japan.

I went here and there to see these things with my own eyes. Does anyone remember nowadays the system of priorities in air travel? With every plane crowded, anyone holding a higher priority could wait at an airport, and on the arrival of a plane destined for the place he was ordered to, could 'bump off' some unfortunate with a lower priority, and fly off happily, leaving his miserable victim waiting disconsolate – perhaps for days – for the chance to board another plane. And in wartime Washington society this priority was the exact, vital measure of personal status. At all the innumerable parties deft questioning was directed to discovering other people's priorities, and I had a No. 2, like four-star generals and admirals, and was treated with corresponding respect. That was not nearly so pleasant as it was to go to sea again, and to discover – what should have been obvious – that with my handicap I could still live on board a ship of war as long as it was no bigger than a destroyer; the distances in a carrier were quite beyond me. There was an occasion (of subsequent importance) when my ship passed through the tail of a typhoon and I experienced the worst weather I had ever seen at sea.

Hornblower had no chance of asserting himself in those conditions; but those minor and seemingly unrelated experiences were, I fancy, storing themselves away in my subconscious even while I toiled at writing the articles about the war in the Pacific – not very good ones; logistics for the common man – while Germany fell and while I was preparing to join the British naval force in the Pacific. And then the war ended, and there was Hornblower demanding attention in a way that could not be denied.

I had been preoccupied with the fall of empires – Hornblower would have recovered from his attack of typhus just in time to be available when the French Empire was falling. There were the political considerations, the peace conferences, the question of a new government for France – as well as for Japan. There had been the crack-up of Mussolini's power under Allied attack;

Hornblower had seen in the last days of the Empire the interesting secession of Bordeaux from Imperial rule. I often had wondered – somehow my reading had never led me to the discovery – what had happened to the Royalist Mayor of Bordeaux, Lynch, when Bonaparte returned to power during the Hundred Days. A great many people during that wild moment must have discovered that they had backed the wrong horse.

These considerations were more urgent in my mind because at the same time as the Nuremberg Trials the trials of the misguided traitors, Lord Haw-Haw and others, were fresh in my memory; I did not remember reading anywhere that, after the fall of the French Empire, England instituted any intense pursuit of the numerous deserters, even traitors, who must have hidden trembling in France awaiting apprehension. Now what really happened to men of this sort at that period? The mutineers of the *Hermione*, a generation earlier, had been hunted down and hanged without mercy. And, of course, what happened to the Comte de Graçay and his daughter-in-law Marie, when Bonaparte during the Hundred Days had them in his power and was aware of the assistance they had given to Hornblower? And Hornblower? With the least pull from the front or push from behind he would plunge again into his affair with Marie. He could certainly, in that case, find himself in a difficult situation during the Hundred Days. Previous to that he must have played an important part in contributing to the fall of the Empire. And those mutineers?

There presented itself in my mind the problem – an interesting mental exercise – of how to deal with a crew of mutineers who had seized their ship and threatened (as had once or twice happened in history) to hand her over to the enemy unless given a promise of immunity. Fight them? Impossible, if the mutineers chose their cruising ground with care. It was amusing – not quite the right word, that; stimulating was a better one – to work out a plan which might be successful. Then there was that storm; I would like to find Hornblower at sea again, contending with dirty weather. And there was the peace-making, and the remodelling of Europe at the Congress of Vienna. Wellington attended that as Ambassador Extraordinary; surely his only sister, if not his brother-in-law, would be involved too, especially as it was notorious that Wellington was not on the best of terms with his Duchess? And Marie de Graçay, to whom I had nearly lost my heart? Earthy and yet sweet; intuitive as well as shrewd; sensible as well as generous; what, if anything, did the future hold for her?

It was a strange jumble of ideas as well as emotions, but there was a solid scaffolding of actual history to provide framework with which to build from these assorted materials. The two systems of construction discussed in Chapter 2 were available simultaneously this time; there were the deeds to be done and yet here were the doers already at hand, and luckily the two methods were mutually self-supporting instead of antagonistic. Things fell into place, and the moment came, and I was off again into a world of Channel gales, and petty but tiresome disagreements between Hornblower and Barbara, and black contrasting tragedy, and moments of profane love balanced against an idyllic village wedding, with Hornblower climbing to the uttermost peak of professional recognition while suffering intense personal loss. War has many dreadful aspects; people are killed in war, and the survivors are changed people – brief words, but charged with tragedy.

But now Lord Hornblower was finished, and I could return to my own world. This is the moment perhaps for me to insert one more personal note; if I were ever to be asked (and, obviously, even without being asked) what was the best ten minutes' work I had ever done, which page of all the thousands I have written displeases me least, I should single out the last, concluding page of *Lord Hornblower* – a complexity of action and emotion expressed as nearly exactly, in the most economical and fitting wording, as I believe I could ever be capable of.

31

Now, with sincere reluctance, I have to allow my physical health to intrude again into this account of the writing of Hornblower, the *enfant terrible* breaking into the polite conversation of his betters. Some years had gone by; other novels had demanded my attention, and (of course) life had been lived between them. Then, suddenly, life nearly left off. The heart attack struck at two in the morning; a coronary occlusion of a severe type, extremely painful. Fortunately my yells for help attracted attention; and Dr Fox, in the best traditions of his profession, instantly turned out of his bed and drove along foggy roads to the rescue. I knew, after the first few seconds, what had happened to me; one of my closest friends had died, three months before, within an hour of experiencing a coronary occlusion. There was time to review the situation, to recall with fair satisfaction that my will was made and my affairs in some sort of order. There were the most bitter regrets, naturally – regrets at leaving this pleasant life, sharpened by thinking about all the things I had not done, and even sharpened by the thought of all the half-formed ideas which I would not have the chance to develop to completion.

Here was Dr Fox standing at my side; little need to tell him what was the matter with me. The pain was severe, and I was shifting my position in bed in the endeavour to find a posture less uncomfortable – it was then that I suddenly realized, with singular clarity, that what I was actually doing was writhing in agony. I had seen it before, both in men and in animals, but I had never writhed in agony myself and it had not occurred to me that I should ever do so. With the realization I tried to lie still; without overmuch success. The needle went in and the plunger was pushed home. 'Aren't you *ever* going to react?' asked Dr Fox, turning back from the telephone after calling for an ambulance. Then the reaction came, the blessed relief of morphine, the dulling of the pain and the lifting of anxiety. Pink clouds of positive (even though unexplainable) happiness began to billow round my bedside. And out of the clouds came three words. I am quite certain that Dr Fox did not utter them – they were much too unprofessional – nor did anyone else at my bedside. But the three words formed in my mind as clearly as if I had heard them. An Even Chance. That was it; an even chance. In the happy illogicality of morphine those words could even raise a smile.

In came the ambulance men with their stretcher, and I was carried out into the night, the pink clouds rolling along beside me and those three words somehow following me up, all the way to the hospital. Weeks of compulsory helplessness followed (I believe nowadays they treat coronary occlusion with less ceremony), accompanied by prolonged struggles to breathe in an oxygen tent, and bewildered efforts to think logically and deal with mundane affairs while the thinking apparatus was clogged by soothing drugs.

Clarity came back accompanied, naturally, by boredom, and for perhaps the last week there was every opportunity to think, and little else to do; the nice nurses were so easy to tease that the sport soon surfeited – it was too much like shooting sitting birds – and having once worked out mentally that I could have exchanged this hospital room for a suite de luxe in the *Queen Mary* (or the wing of an oriental palace complete with dancers) and still be money in hand, there was the tendency to think about other matters. It was still too physically tiring to hold up a book for long; thought it had to be.

32

THERE was that queer memory about the even chance. Perhaps it had been my own subconscious estimate of my chance of survival. Possibly it was a breaking through from down below of the germ of a story too young to be recognized for what it was – a sudden bobbing up of a waterlogged timber bearing an immature barnacle, under the stimulus of morphine. But there was the phrase, and inevitably it began to sprout, upward and down, as a seed will send out shoots.

It was a phrase which might perhaps apply to a duel. No, it would not. All the rules and etiquette of the duel were directed towards eliminating chance, towards making sure that the more skilful would not suffer as the result of accidental circumstances. The measurement of swords, the choosing of even ground, all this had a specious appearance of trying to be fair, but actually it really meant that the better shot, or the better swordsman, had a better chance, in a matter of honour which really had nothing to do with marksmanship or skill in fencing. An inexperienced duellist with a grievance might well complain at the dice being weighted against him like this. He might seek to give himself a chance – an even chance.

So there grew up in the mind the picture of someone so angry, or so un-happy, that he would be willing to risk his life if in exchange he had an even chance of putting an end to his troubles. Most likely that would be a young man – it has been observed ever since civilization (and formalized murder) began that young men, with far more to lose, are the more ready to risk losing it. A young man, suffering from intense troubles which he could directly attribute to one other man, presumably also young. A schoolboy might feel that way, except that duelling was unusual among schoolboys.

But a midshipman in the old navy – horrible things went on in the midship-men's mess in the old days, and duels were frequent enough to be not unusual. Someone might easily make a mathematical calculation, weighing an even chance of survival against the certainty that his misery was otherwise incurable. A mathematical calculation! Now whom did I know, and on whom had I once (in a fit of self-indulgence) bestowed a mathematical talent? The answer did not even have to be put into words. All that I knew about the later Horn-blower seemed to fit in with the picture of the younger Hornblower who began to grow up in my mind. And the later one was such a diversified character that it would be fun to work out how he came to grow up like that.

All this was a major development, clearly. Hornblower had been out of my thoughts for years; I had taken him to the top of the tree and left him there – not too comfortably – with every intention of never looking back at him. There were dozens of other projects in my mind, dozens of other eggs hatching in the nest, and I was extremely doubtful about introducing this sort of cuckoo. I left the hospital, so that all the projects came to be forgotten in the excitement of learning to live again.

117

33

THIS odd profession of mine has brought me a great deal of happiness, even though I feel shamefaced about confessing it. That was a remarkably happy period, up in the clear, delightful air of the High Sierra, which – so the cliché runs – is like champagne. Perhaps because of that the ideas came bubbling up as well. The gangling, thoughtful youth who was taking shape in my mind began to win my affection – he was inclined to take things over-seriously, and yet he was learning to laugh; he had a great deal of ability, and his addiction to self-analysis called his attention to his own weaknesses so that he would make the effort to eliminate them, or at least render them ineffective, and that would enable him to profit by the intensive training given a young officer in those busy days.

Busy days they could certainly be, with those ideas bubbling up in endless succession. That duel with the even chance could easily lead to transfer to a more lively field of endeavour, with plenty of activity. In 1794 there was commerce destruction in the Bay of Biscay; absurdly young officers frequently found themselves called upon to navigate prizes back to home ports – and here was the idea of a cargo of rice swelling up because of a leak. His rather solemn priggishness could lead to his condemning himself to the penalty of failure. In early 1795 there was the disastrous expedition to Quiberon; in 1796 would come – as so often in history – a change of sides by the Spanish Government, leading, of course (while I was cautiously rowing a boat over the blue waters of Fallen Leaf Lake) to a skirmish with the Spanish galleys that still survived centuries of nautical development.

There were endless things that could happen, and yet not quite endless. Cassandralike, I was aware of the doom that awaited Hornblower. A dozen years before, that doom had been pronounced. He was going to be taken prisoner by the Spaniards, because he had to learn the Spanish language so that in 1808 he would be able to converse with El Supremo. But that imprisonment must not hinder this advancement, so that it must come to an end long before the natural end at the Peace of Amiens in 1801. Capture was easily arranged – he could be carrying dispatches in a small vessel and, through no fault of his own, he could fall into the hands of the Spanish fleet at sea before the Battle of Cape St Vincent in 1797. This very misfortune could be used to help along his necessary promotion to lieutenant. But then he must be set free in some way. Escape? Oddly, he had escaped from imprisonment once already – true, that was a dozen years later, in 1810, but we could not have him doing so again in 1798. Some distinctive reason had to be thought up that would give good grounds for his regaining his freedom. There was singularly little trouble about thinking out the necessary mechanism; that was really too strong an expression – it sufficed to realize the necessity, and the solution presented itself. It was almost worth having had weeks in a hospital bed if afterwards the mind worked so readily.

Naturally, there was nothing to do except to write all this. It was going to be quite easy because the stories had presented themselves as separate episodes, so that a sensible man would be able to write one and then stop and recover before starting the next. In fact, it was most convenient that this should be so, with a coronary occlusion not so far in the past. Sheer nonsense, of course. With each story bubbling up from below the instant the dead weight of its predecessor was lifted from it, it was impossible to hold back from starting again. There was always that will o' the wisp – this story is not as good as I hoped it was going to be, but I am quite sure this next one will be. So story after story flowed from my pen, each one begun in hope, and it was not true that each was finished in despair – the next one was demanding too much attention for any thought to be given to the last.

Partly because of this, but largely because of other circumstances, the act of writing was not quite as laborious as usual. There was a genuine pleasure in watching my young man growing up, acquiring some sense and some ballast. In the tense sessions of visualization I was going along with a young fellow to whom everything was new, who enjoyed all the resilience of youth – it was ridiculous, but true, that he could confer some of it on me. Lastly, there was satisfaction in achievement; the parts were falling into place. If I had ever stopped to think beforehand, I might have contemplated with dismay the necessity for creating a youth who had to grow into someone already well understood in his prime, but that difficulty had really never occurred to me in the excitement of the moment – the thought had merely been added spice to the prospective dish – and it was only later that I could look back on it and grudgingly agree that at least it had been something worth attempting.

34

THERE was other work to be done when the *Midshipman* was finished; there was life to be lived, possibly more urgently still, as a result of recent events. Hornblower was now some sort of public figure. He had made me innumerable friends. On a dozen different frontiers I could arrive with my baggage and present myself to a customs officer, and, with my name noted, the officer would say 'Not—?' and I would say 'Yes,' and my baggage would be instantly chalked or labelled or waved through. Hornblower was a kind of perpetual travelling companion, even though he was far removed from the new thoughts that occupied my mind regarding my new work. Letters came in steadily; and a surprising proportion of them demanded more news of Hornblower. Letters from readers are frequently what I call 'but' letters – 'I liked your book but—'; yet these were mostly friendly letters. I do not believe they exerted any direct influence on me; except as a wartime duty I had never written a word I did not want to write, and the only person I have ever attempted to please by my work is me – or I, if it is necessary to be grammatical. Yet when every mail delivery brought letters like that; when I could hardly ever have conversations with acquaintances (friends came to know me better) without Hornblower's name coming up in the opening sentences, it was hard to keep him entirely out of my mind. That is a practical explanation of why it all started again, but there were other factors.

There was the continual lure of trying to explain Hornblower's marriage to Maria. All those years back in *The Happy Return* it had been easy, and I believe not inconsistent, to pass it off as one of those things that happen to people, but an actual word-for-word description of the process was tempting in its difficulty. Technical problems have their allure; they are most definitely seductive. And – here comes the confession – I wanted to know, I wanted to find out the details for myself, I wanted to work out how it came about.

There crept up in my memory pictures of another young man, incredibly lean and lantern-jawed and earnest, who through an unfriendly winter had spent his days writing *Payment Deferred* and his nights in playing bridge professionally, who ate well when the cards came his way and remarkably poorly when they did not. I remembered that young man very well indeed; it was as if he were a friend of my youth who had died years ago, and I suppose he really was dead, and the present me inhabited the changed body he had left behind. It was interesting how those memories haunted me.

Another problem. Hornblower had emerged from his midshipman's chrysalis to become a lieutenant. But how had it happened that he had received his next step to commander, over the heads of hundreds of his seniors? How had it happened without his achieving a blaze of glory? How *could* it happen in a way that would leave Hornblower the rather cynical and dissatisfied individual he developed into? Time flies; in 1808 he was a captain of some years' seniority – much would have to be crammed into the intervening years, and those events would have to have a special and particular quality. Besides, there was the Peace of Amiens to be considered – nearly two years of peacetime without any chance of achieving distinction. Two years probably of half pay – and we already knew that Hornblower was a whist player of merit.

Something also happened – something as hard to explain as any of these. How did the *Artillery Manual* for the British Militia for 1860 ever arrive in a second-hand bookshop in San Francisco? A copy certainly showed up there, because I bought it. In 1860 the British militia was concerned about the possibility of invasion by the armies of Napoleon III, but their artillerymen still manned guns exactly like those that were used against Napoleon I. And the special concern of militia artillery was coastal defence, and coastal defence against wooden ships – the day of the ironclad was only just beginning to dawn. What the artillery militia proposed to use was red-hot shot, the same as had been used in the defence of Gibraltar nearly a century earlier. A good half of the manual was devoted to the drill for the employment of red-hot shot – it was a drill that had to be carried out very punctiliously, with lumps of red-hot metal being carried about amid barrels of gunpowder. That *Artillery Manual* made good bedside reading for several nights; I had never before studied details of the handling of red-hot shot. It was a remarkably substantial morsel to come within reach of the jellyfish's tentacles.

There was another point. If ever – as was most unlikely – I were to write about Hornblower again, and deal with this portion of his life ending in his marriage, it would be desirable – necessary – to write from another angle. That was what my taste or judgment dictated to me, in a way which, as in most matters of taste, is more easily felt than described. Someone had to observe Hornblower's future wife more objectively than Hornblower himself could be expected to do. For that matter it was time that Hornblower himself was put through an objective examination. This, if ever, would be the right moment, while Hornblower was still a junior officer and subject to command. And, of course, as soon as that decision was reached the writing of the book became more desirable still, because of the added attraction of the difficult technical problems it would present. The right moment; there was pleasure in admitting that phrase into my thoughts.

Somehow, at this time another fragment of a plot made its reappearance. There was the question of a mad captain; junior officers in a ship, and especially a ship of war, find themselves in a terribly difficult position when they have reason to believe their captain is insane; my attention had been pointedly called to this two years before, when thinking about the mutineers in *Lord Hornblower*. Under the Articles of War any discussion between even two men regarding their dissatisfaction with some aspect of their service was mutinous

121

and criminal and liable to terrible punishment. Reading that Article of War had started a train of thought that still nagged and demanded attention.

So there we were; red-hot shot and marriage; promotion and professional card-playing; a mad captain and a different point of view; there were a dozen different elements (I have no doubt there were several which I discarded and have now forgotten) all elbowing each other and trying to push their way into the picture. Luckily, as ever, all I had to do was to be patient. The details sorted themselves out and arranged themselves in order, and I could indulge in daily and unjustified self-congratulation when each morning revealed further progress towards the completion of this process. It was only at the end that I had to intervene personally, to make my own arbitrary decision between rival claimants, to do a little honest work in the matter of studying my sources for confirmation of my theories. Then, at last, it happened. Not only was the course of events clear in my mind but it had been clear for a couple of weeks or so; at that moment I made a series of discoveries about myself. One was that although there was as usual the genuine distaste for plunging into fatiguing work, it was almost counterbalanced by my desire to put my theories into practice, to turn my ideas into words on paper. Worse still, I brought myself up before the stern judge who was myself and found myself guilty of something unheard-of heretofore. I was actually savouring these pleasures in anticipation, and, like a child with a plate of food before him, I was saving up the best until the last, as if the actual writing could be considered as having any desirable aspects at all, let alone being the 'best.' Fortunately I had long ago ceased to be surprised at any new inconsistency I might display. The judge's sentence was, of course, that I should sit myself at my writing pad on the spot, and sure enough, it only called for a day or two's real work to dissipate all these odd notions, especially as very early, as soon, in fact, as a minimum amount of work was completed, the old bogy presented itself – the fear that I might die with the book incomplete, with the final developments never to be revealed. That, more than any other consideration, drove me to write the book in the usual desperate haste burningly anxious to show Hornblower in his cross-grained moods, by refusing to rejoice in his own successes, refusing to truckle to authority when truckling was obviously called for and might be exceedingly profitable, and, above all, by allowing his silly temperament to draw him into a silly marriage, all this under the puzzled eyes of his friend Bush.

35

INEVITABLY, I suppose, it all happened again, this time after a much smaller interval than of late; about eighteen months, in fact – a period spent in all sorts of activities, from a prolonged visit to the West Indies to writing a minor history textbook for children. Here were the ideas creeping in again. Someone gave me a vivid account of the methods of the pearl divers of Ceylon in the old days. Something else again; it may have been with advancing years that my own memories of past experiences kept returning with renewed clarity; once I had taken a motor-boat clear across England and back again, from London to Llangollen, by canal, and I frequently found myself recalling incidents in that peculiar voyage. On another occasion I had had to navigate a small boat on a stormy day through London, up from the Pool, through wild river traffic – that voyage ended in disaster at Vauxhall Bridge, with safety almost in sight.

Seeing that the Hornblower novels always were about Hornblower (another statement of the obvious) it was interesting that, to a great extent, the old method prevailed of thinking first of the thing to be done and then selecting the right person to do the deed. It was a coincidence (is that the whole truth? I fear I am not being entirely honest, even while trying to be) that the right person should turn out to be Hornblower. The bare bones of history constituted, appropriately, a skeleton framework on which a story could be constructed. Hornblower must have been 'made post,' promoted to captain, sometime in the spring of 1805; October, 1805 saw the battle of Trafalgar, and the following January saw Nelson's funeral procession up the Thames from Greenwich to Whitehall. There were plenty of accounts of this extraordinary display; there were numerous contemporary prints to illustrate them. I knew from personal experience what the Thames was like on a bad day – those ceremonial barges must have been horribly difficult to handle. There was the mischievous notion that perhaps the barge containing Nelson's coffin might have sunk in mid-procession. And what would be more natural than that Hornblower, a very junior captain, should be given the duty of organizing the procession? It would be onerous, highly responsible, and devoid of glory – certainly it was a duty that would be thrust upon the captain least able to evade it. Hornblower would be posted to a very small ship – small enough to be fitted out in the river at Deptford, so that he would be on the spot, readily available. Fitting out for what mission? What about those pearl divers?

So the development was instantly in full swing. By what route had he come to London? By canal, of course – somewhere or other I had read about the express passenger service that was maintained on the canals during their brief heyday before the coming of railways. Maria would certainly accompany him. But here were the germs of tragedy. Fifteen years ago, as mentioned in *The Happy Return*, but two years in the future as regards the present Hornblower, his two children died of smallpox. Here were chickens coming home to roost; the comparison must be made, despite the frivolity of that wording when applied to the horrible truth. The children had to be born, they had to bring Hornblower some brief happiness, and they had to die. The dates served, very fortunately; Hornblower's marriage was in April, 1803, and here we were in January, 1806. Time enough for two pregnancies. But those pearl divers?

And *The Happy Return* had found Hornblower with a sword of honour presented him by the Patriotic Fund for boarding the *Castilla*; it was certainly time that he should board the *Castilla* and win that sword, pearl divers or no pearl divers. And time was hurrying by; the summer of 1808 was to find him in command of the *Lydia* in the Gulf of Fonseca. There was plenty to be done, especially as somewhere about this time my attention had been called to the Continental usage of putting a crossbar on the figure 7 when writing it. That had to be attended to somehow; also how did it happen that Hornblower was transferred from his present ship – name unknown at the moment – to the *Lydia* in a way that would help to give some bitterness to his temperament?

It was a delightful life, sitting back and letting these tangles sort themselves out. There was that tour of the West Indies, flying from island to island, chartering a motor car in each, and driving up into the innermost recesses through enchanted forests or barren hills. Those islands were fiercely insistent upon displaying their freedom from ordinary international convention; an international driving licence meant nothing to them – I had to pass a dozen different driving tests and earn a dozen different licences, which I really believe helped those pearl divers to come to life; construction is an odd business. Then home again, to the familiar work-table and the familiar fatigue. My method of visualization while writing has its disadvantages; tragedy strikes the harder. I had to kill two children. It was on the last page of the manuscript that they died, leaving Maria heartbroken and Hornblower desolate. I can remember sitting with the final words written, feeling not exactly heartbroken, but certainly desolate, and most desperately sorry that I had had to do that to Hornblower.

36

So it seemed as if the cycle of novels was now complete. Owing to my light-hearted beginning of *Hornblower and the Atropos* in late 1805 there was a gap of two and a half years during which Hornblower must have gained promotion from commander, but, except for that, his career had been described throughout the period of the French Wars, from the declaration in 1793 to Waterloo in 1815, and I could look upon this aspect of my work as completed, and I thought (vain thoughts) that now I could call my soul my own. I could do the other work I had long been anxious to do. The rough with the smooth; there was a nightmare period of reading the evidence given at the Nuremberg trials – a casual turning of the pages of the interminable volumes was like the first step into quicksand. There was a novel about the United States Navy in action which I had long been anxious to write; with Hornblower out of the way it demanded my attention in the usual fashion. There was sober history to be written, and – as I have pointed out before, perhaps without laying sufficient stress upon it – there was life to be lived. There was an interval of sailing a yacht in the Caribbean, to fall once more under the spell of the West Indies. There was a moment when I clumsily drove a motor car over a small precipice in Mexico, and had to spend some days (they might have been weary days, but of course proved not to be) in the earthquake-shattered city of Colima; it had not been much of a city before the earthquake. There was this to be done, and that to be done, and something else to be thought about. Anyone might have believed that Hornblower would have left me alone now, with all these preoccupations, happy and otherwise, but he would not. Perhaps I can blame it on my correspondents, who would not let him rest; two or three times each week at least there came letters asking for news of him; certainly that kept him in my mind when I might otherwise have forgotten about him. I was even moved to write a ballade abusing him – the vital line was 'I hope you roast in hell, Horatio' – which was not merely published but paid for; I had written almost no verse since my discovery at the age of twenty that (for me, at least) prose was a more suitable medium.

Needless to say, the ideas began to creep in. The first impulse came when I found myself wondering about Hornblower and his Barbara. I came to the conclusion that after the frightful tragedy of Marie de Graçay, and his own terrifying experience, Hornblower must have gone back with considerable relief to Barbara, who, undoubtedly, would have enough understanding and kindness to make him welcome. I could well imagine it; I could imagine those two proud people, both of them reluctant to merge their personalities, finding that such a thing was at least possible, with mutual respect coming to reinforce mutual attraction. But Hornblower was never a man to know complete happiness, and he was the kind of cross-grained individual who would distrust it when it was waiting for him. Barbara had been married once before; it would be just like Hornblower to brood about that, to allow his vivid imagination to conjure up mental pictures that would rouse a feeling of jealousy, to confuse the flesh and the spirit, the past and the present, if only to provide a base on which to build a new discontent. Undoubtedly that would be just like Hornblower; fortunately Barbara would be discerning enough to be aware of it, and tactful and clever enough to keep the discontent down to a minimum.

This was a small enough germ to begin with, but of course others made their appearance. Hornblower would fret if he never saw service again. He had been 'made post' in the spring of 1805; the usual miraculous coincidence came to my assistance here, for that made him senior to all the captains who attained that rank in the spate of promotion following Trafalgar. He would probably attain flag rank in 1820 or 1821, and with his record he could count with some assurance of employment even in the attenuated navy of those lean years. It was an interesting coincidence that Napoleon died in 1821. The Spanish empire was still breaking up at that time; that was another interesting coincidence, seeing that it was the beginning of that convulsion which had called Hornblower into existence in 1808 – or 1936, to use another reckoning. There was plenty of fighting going on in Mexico and Central and South America at the time Hornblower would be promoted to rear admiral, while the Royal Navy kept the ring and the United States put forward the Monroe Doctrine. There was the suppression of the slave trade, too – the Royal Navy had undertaken the enforcement, and the Spanish and Portuguese colonies constituted the main market for the trade. Undoubtedly, if Hornblower were to be employed, it would be in the West Indies.

What would he be like? What sort of a man would he have grown into? His peerage and his flag would do something to mellow him, surely, however much he would distrust distinctions that he had not conferred on himself. But even though mellowed he would not lose his old restlessness, his desire for action, his quickness of thought. He would be witnessing rapid changes at sea, the development of the clipper ship, the beginnings of steam, and he was a liberal-minded man who would not be in accord with the conservative attitude of the navy towards these innovations. For me, there was a great deal of appeal about these considerations; down in my subconscious ideas were struggling towards maturity. In Jamaica to this day there is a small area – the Cockpit

Country – still inaccessible, still the scene of a different culture, whose impassable boundary is hardly half an hour's drive from the glittering palaces of Montego Bay. I had gazed down into it myself, repeatedly, from precarious roads on rainswept hillsides. The Cockpit Country began to haunt me.

Somewhere or other – I have quite forgotten where – I came across a curious historical item; after Waterloo a large number of Napoleon's Old Guard had organized themselves into an association that had seized, and attempted to colonize, an area of Texas, at a time when Texas was still part of Mexico and Mexico was still fighting for her independence. What was likely to happen to them? There was room for conjecture – and I must remember that Napoleon's death occurred about that time. And all sorts of hotheads, from all sorts of motives, came to take part in the struggle for independence. I could picture some of them; I could picture Hornblower's attitude towards them, both official and personal. But I must not overlook, among all these distractions, the original wonderings about the relationship between Hornblower and Barbara.

Now a woman comes into this story, a real flesh-and-blood woman, not a mere character in a novel like Barbara and Marie and Maria. Flesh and blood, but really a saint – a truly good woman, so good that I dare, without permission, to tell this story about her and still hope for forgiveness. A saint with one pardonable weakness, and that is a complete inability to resist the appeal of flowers. The streets in Californian cities in the springtime are made beautiful by flowering trees, in hundreds, in thousands. How could anyone resist the temptation to snip off a few sprays so as to make flower arrangements? How could anyone resist? Nearly everyone does, as far as I know, except my saintly friend. Of course it is against the law, and so I have made up my own version of the story of the miracle of St Elizabeth of Hungary. My friend is out with her secateurs and her little bag, snip-snip-snipping. Up drives a policeman. 'What is in that bag?' he asks. 'Only groceries,' replies the poor little saint. 'Show me,' says the policeman. And she opens her bag, and, of course, it is full of groceries.

It was odd how that story haunted me. Then it began, the old familiar stirring of the emotions, the feeling of recognition, the knowledge that something was about to take shape. And so it did – with everything coming at once. That had happened before, and would happen again. I do not understand why it is, that when I am constructing a story which is quite episodic, the episodes should all take form at once, or as nearly as my capacity allows. One day all the episodes are chaotic, formless, and then on a later day, not so long afterwards, they have all taken shape and are arranging themselves in order – I had had the same experience with the *Midshipman* as well as with other books.

There have been occasions when psychologists have questioned me to discover the mechanism of these processes. They call them 'creative,' but that is a misnomer; the eventual result is creation, if such a self-satisfied word can be tolerated, but the processes are to a large extent – are almost entirely – involuntary. Does a chicken lay an egg because she wants to or because she has to? Just possibly the writer may assist, or speed up, his processes by making himself receptive, by offering hospitality to the wandering idea, but I not only do not believe it but I am inclined to think the opposite is true. Certainly there is a danger point at which there is a sharp transition between being receptive and trying to force the process; if ideas are forced the result is nearly always – let us say invariably – hackneyed or unnatural or pedantic. The average Hollywood story conference is a deliberate attempt to force the formation of ideas.

So far in my life I have flinched from going more deeply into this question; when the psychologists have started to probe I have always remembered how easy it is to take a watch to pieces and how hard it is to make it go again. Maybe my ideas come because, deeply rooted, there is something wrong with me, which analysis might cure. If this is so I cannot think of a better example of the remedy being worse than the disease. I have no desire whatever to be cured of something which has piled interest into my life from boyhood until now, and I hardly expect to grow so old that I shall decide that there is sufficiently little in the future to lose, and submit to analysis to discover the cause of the flow.

A few paragraphs back *Hornblower in the West Indies* had just formed itself in my mind, and from there to the writing it was only a step – the usual step onto the toboggan slide. Precipitately the stories ran on; is it of any interest that in my opinion the story about Hornblower and St Elizabeth of Hungary (which owes its existence to my flower-snipping friend) is the best story I have ever written? My opinion may be of academic interest, at least. As a digression I may mention that it was in the middle of that story that a Hollywood producer telephoned to me. I will not give his name, but it may be sufficient to add that he was of Greek extraction. Plans were forming, he said, to make a film about the sinking of the German battleship *Bismarck*, and would I help? It would have been a tempting invitation from every point of view, except that I was well started on the book and quite immune to temptation. There is nobody in the world less like a bulldog than myself, I suppose – except in this one respect. Once my teeth are clenched into a piece of work no inducement will make me unclench them – that, again, is nothing to be proud of, any more than the bulldog should be proud of what has been bred into him.

So to the pleadings of Hollywood I turned a deaf ear – that analogy being very close to the truth, for I hardly listened to the arguments, being so preoccupied with my current work. I could only say that I would not be available for another two months. No, I was not under contract to anyone else. Yes, I liked the idea, but I simply could not leave off what I was doing. If the need was urgent (as Hollywood needs always appear to be) they had better get someone else. Good-bye.

When I hung up the telephone I thought about the Greek extraction of the producer to whom I had been talking, and I remembered the story about Archimedes. He had been prominent in the defence of Syracuse against the Romans, and when the city was stormed, Marcellus, the Roman commander, gave orders that he was to be taken alive. But Archimedes was deep in some geometrical problem, and only gave an angry answer when a Roman soldier interrupted him to ask who he was, and so the soldier killed him. It seemed as if I had acted in the same way.

Of course Hollywood had not been in nearly so much of a hurry as Hollywood had believed itself to be, and two and a half months later I walked into the first conference that eventually resulted in the filming of *Sink the Bismarck*. There the producer hugged me like a bear (he rather resembled a bear) and said (to my utter astonishment and delight) 'I'm glad to meet you, Archimedes.' Nowadays in my mind St Elizabeth of Hungary is not only associated with my saintly friend, and with Hornblower's pursuit of Cambronne down the Caribbean, but also with the *Bismarck* and with Archimedes – the sort of mixed association which sometimes gives rise to plots, although none has made its appearance in this connection so far – unless this is it.

37

THERE was that gap in Hornblower's life, between the renewal of war in 1803 and his appearance on the Thames-Severn canal in 1805. It was really remarkable how many correspondents wrote to me and pointed it out – but, as before, I cannot lay the blame for the result on the shoulders of the kindly people who wrote to me. I was intrigued about that gap myself, even though I had not given it a thought when I began to write the *Atropos*. Now, not quite against my will, I found myself working out what must have happened. I had left him on the verge of getting married, newly promoted to commander, and about to serve in the renewed war; on his next appearance he was a captain and the father of a child with another one about to be born. So certain points were settled for me without any need for invention. He had distinguished himself – although that could have been taken for granted in any case, seeing that Hornblower was Hornblower; and also because there had to be a story about him. He must have been home on leave, too, to account for that second child, and that was by no means the general rule in the old navy.

The explanation was obvious; he must have served in the fleet blockading Brest – the ships of that squadron frequently had to put back into home ports to refit when damaged. As he was a commander his ship would be a small, light vessel – the kind of ship that would be employed in close observation of Brest; plenty of opportunity to gain distinction, then, and plenty of chance to receive damage compelling a return to port, even though Cornwallis in command was chary about giving permission to return. And so construction was off to a flying start.

One point to bear in mind. Hornblower, in later life, had been notoriously unlucky in the matter of prize money, so that however much he was to distinguish himself at Brest he was not to capture prizes; the ships he was to fight must either be destroyed or must escape. Unless – a sudden memory sent me hurrying to my history books. There it was. The incident of the captured Spanish treasure fleet, which convulsed with mirth the whole Royal Navy except for the participants, had occurred in the autumn of 1804, just when Hornblower could have taken part in it. That was one more of the convenient coincidences which studded Hornblower's paper career; I can be quite conscienceless about history if it is necessary – I might have made use of the treasure fleet incident even if it had actually occurred in 1801 or 1807 – but as it was I was not even put to the test. The actual course of events fitted exactly into *Hornblower and the Hotspur* without any straining – an imitation of Art by Nature that might have delighted the heart of Oscar Wilde.

Relative to this subject I might mention as an aside something I forgot to mention when I was dealing with the *Commodore,* for in the writing of that book I imperilled – almost ended – a valued friendship. For an eminent historian – a friend for years – wrote to me on reading *The Commodore:* 'I knew there were British forces engaged at the siege of Riga, but I have never been able to find out much about them. What were your sources?' I could only reply lamely that I had no sources, that I had decided that Riga could not have been besieged without British forces arriving to help, and Hornblower (as usual) had been handy. No one would believe, without reading the letter I received in reply, how hard was the rap on the knuckles that historian administered to me. It smarts to this day, even though I know it was undeserved.

There were some cheerless aspects about the usually pleasant work of construction. There was poor Maria; here she was on her honeymoon, entering into married life, having children. I knew the fate in store for her, and the fate in store for those children. Surely now I could impart a little joy into her otherwise joyless life? Almost none. There was a war on; Hornblower was serving in the Channel Fleet; and Hornblower was Hornblower. In the face of that combination of circumstances there was little that I could do for her. At least I saved her from disillusionment, I could help her in a negative kind of way, but I could not allow sentiment to spoil the story. Already we knew the sort of man Hornblower was to grow into; already we knew how the marriage was to develop. There was a Calvinistic predestination about the whole affair; for that matter the moving finger had already written. Maria was a butterfly (was there ever anyone quite so un-butterfly-like?) crushed between the grinding surfaces of fact and fiction.

38

ANOTHER thing I have not mentioned so far. It is a superstition of mine that dull moments come to an end when construction finishes and I address myself to the task of writing. Presumably during the happy time of construction I am not sensitive to the ordinary small disasters of ordinary life, and when I am writing I am liable to be highly sensitive to them. It always seems to me that the moment I write 'Page One' and start honest work, things begin to happen, and there is never a dull moment. During the writing of *Hotspur* the coincidences were quite uncanny in their occurrence. I had not written half a dozen pages before construction work of another kind began across the road, not fifty yards from the window of my secluded and usually tomb-like workroom. Every pneumatic drill, every concrete mixer, bulldozer, and air compressor in California went to work there. The noise was hideous and ceaseless. In other circumstances I would have moved away, but how could I at that moment? With an effort I could have taken fifty books of reference with me, but only in the certain knowledge that it would be the fifty-first that I would need, when suddenly I would have to have the weight and dimensions of a hogshead of pork, or the maximum range of a French field howitzer. I could only try to lose myself in my visualizations and work on through the noise. While the noise was still going on a friend fell seriously ill, ill enough, and lonely enough, and enough of a friend for my personal intervention to be called for to deal with doctors and hospitals. The ink was hardly dry on the letters I had to write about all this before I lost my secretary and had to find another; the truest words Abraham Lincoln ever said were those warning against changing secretaries while writing a novel. Then, as if they had been waiting for the perfect moment, Internal Revenue leaped upon me with a request for a special investigation, demanding facts about my sources of income that I never had troubled to know and that the new secretary could not possibly know, and morning after morning I had to get up dazed from my desk, leaving Hornblower at grips with French frigates, and answer questions about matters of which I knew even less than I knew (as I remarked earlier in this book) about harmony and counterpoint. The providence that looks after sleepwalkers and drunkards came to my rescue, and I can proudly boast that I am one of the few men who have emerged from a special investigation with the Internal Revenue owing me money instead of the other way about. If I had not been so involved with the *Hotspur* I should have had that final letter from Internal Revenue framed and hung on my workroom wall – I still have not had time to arrange for that.

All this was during the summer months, and it is mostly during the summer months that visitors come to stay. Never has my house been so full of visitors as it was while I was writing *Hotspur* and training a new secretary and dealing with Internal Revenue and the hospitals. Friends were sleeping everywhere – there was a period when a charming young woman was sleeping on a hired bed made up in my workroom, and sleeping late, as young women will, so that I had to turn her out of bed each morning before I could settle down and sail with Hornblower to attack the Spanish *flota*. It seemed as if we could never manage to sit down with less than six to lunch and eight to dinner, all very light-hearted except for me; because of Hornblower and Maria – and perhaps because of Internal Revenue – I was a skeleton at fifty feasts during that lively time.

Despite all these handicaps there was an additional and weighty reason for finishing the book. Not only had I made my usual promises of delivery, and not only was I in my usual condition of panic awaiting the end, but also I was due to make a journey round the world. The reservations were all made, the passages all booked, and in a tiny area in southern Portugal the hoop-petti-coated daffodil was due to bloom in the early spring, ten thousand miles away, and I was anxious to arrive there at exactly the right moment, even though to the unprejudiced eye the hoop-petticoated daffodil (one of the great aunts of the cultivated daffodil) is a miserable object barely two inches tall and not worth crossing the street for, to say nothing of going round the world for.

So *Hotspur* simply had to be finished; it did not surprise me in the least to discover that the full development of the story called for more words than I had calculated upon at the start. I had left ten days in reserve, and nine of them were consumed in dealing with Hornblower's promotion to captain. So that the day the typescripts were put into the post and started off eastward to the publishers, I started off westward to the hoop-petticoated daffodil via New Zealand. There was not even time for the usual feeling of disappointment; there was hardly time for the realization to sink in that I had finished with Hornblower for good and all.

39

It was sixteen months ago that I wrote the last words of *Hotspur*. Of course Hornblower has troubled me since then, occasionally. It might be thought that with all the gaps in his active life filled up there would be no chance for invention to find anything to work on, and yet it does. Here is an example, which I am writing to show how a story presents itself to my mind, ready to be written. I am curious, myself, to see how the next paragraph or two will appear when completed (I can hardly guess), because I suppose that if ever I were to write preliminary notes they would take this as yet undetermined form.

The story is called *The Point and the Edge*. The time is 1819, with Hornblower a senior captain on half pay. His restlessness, as always, demands exercise, and he has been for long taking fencing lessons; his memories of a dozen hand-to-hand fights are now coloured by the strengthened realization of how the point will always beat the edge when skilfully used. England at this time is in the depths of a postwar slump; people are starving through lack of employment, and despite the savage laws, which enact that a man may be hanged for the theft of five shillings, crime is rampant. Hornblower has been invited to dine at Portsmouth on the flagship of a friend – say Lord Exmouth – who is fortunate enough to have employment in the exiguous navy that England still maintains. Hornblower travels down with Barbara, and puts up at the George. In the late afternoon Barbara looks him over, sees that his civilian clothes are in good order, that he is wearing his gold watch and chain, and carrying his gold-topped ebony walking-stick, and sees him off, while she spends – like a dutiful wife – a dull evening alone.

Exmouth and Hornblower, of course, spend a pleasant evening, discussing the state of the nation and naval policy; Exmouth, rubbing his hands with glee, tells Hornblower of the revolution in recruiting methods nowadays. No flamboyant posters, no press gangs – starving seamen stand in line, waiting for the chance to enlist in the Royal Navy. Captains can pick and choose. Dinner over, Hornblower, fashionable clothes, gold-topped walking-stick and all, starts back to The George. At a dark corner a man springs out at him. He is barefooted, wearing only a tattered shirt and trousers, and starving. In his hand is a branch torn from a tree – his entire stock in trade, his entire working capital. Threatening Hornblower with this improvised club he demands Hornblower's money. This footpad is actually risking his life, risking hanging, for a meal. Hornblower's liberal feelings have no time to assert themselves. He reacts violently against compulsion, and without a thought he lunges with his walking-stick, a quick, instant thrust. The point beats the edge – it lands on the footpad's cheek, half stunning him, so that he reels back momentarily incapacitated. Hornblower cracks him over the wrist so that he drops his club and is at Hornblower's mercy. Hornblower could now call the watch and have this man seized and taken away to certain death, but he naturally cannot bring himself to do so. Instead he drives him before him back to Exmouth's ship. 'My Lord, would you please do me one more favour? Would you be so kind as to enlist this man into your crew?'

There is the completed story – five days of methodical writing and it would be ready for publication. With the usual flurry of excitement it has presented itself in this form, unsought, adapted to this particular period – and only this period – ready for writing. Long novels take shape in exactly the same way, adapting themselves to the times. It has happened scores of times, possibly hundreds of times, in my life, and I still do not know how or why, although the adaptation to the necessary period is explainable, perhaps, because the ideas are necessarily canalized into it.

40

IT is a curious ability to be born with. Like the freaks in the circus sideshows, I earn my living by my freakishness, although with a great deal more physical comfort, I am sure. And – there is no way of evading the conclusion – I have exploited my own freakishness as Barnum and Bailey exploited General Tom Thumb. There is an excuse which I can offer – the same defence as is put forward every day in criminal trials. Undoubtedly there is an irresistible impulse. It is almost impossible, having formulated an idea, to resist putting it on paper, and, once it is on paper, it is just as impossible to resist presenting it to the public.

That was an additional reason for writing about *The Point and the Edge* in the preceding paragraphs. There are other ideas stratified underneath that one – ideas come in groups, as I think I have already mentioned. There might be another book, but what I have just written may – I fancy – head it off and cause it to be unwritten; there are other books I would prefer to write, books with more adventure and difficulty for me personally. That book (now here is another ridiculous reaction) would be too easy.

So perhaps these final paragraphs that I am writing are the last I shall ever write about Hornblower. I have tried to explain all the other Hornblower books, so I must try to explain this present one. It started with the idea of the maps; that idea had been with me for several years. It was remarkably tempting. I wanted to find out if the novels would pass the rather searching test of actual analysis as regards geography as well as history. To gratify my curiosity I was even willing to suffer the discomfort of picking up the novels again and turning the pages over one by one and going through past work while plotting out courses and battle charts. From there it was only a step to remembering the circumstances that caused the books to be written. Most of those memories – as I hope has been apparent – were happy ones, and the decision came to write about them, to resavour the happiness. Just for once I would write a book that needed no planning, no construction. For the actual writing no visualization would be necessary; only a simple recording of facts.

That did not prove to be true; while writing this present book I have had to get up on to the stage and watch the antics of the young man who was me just as I once watched the performances of Hornblower. I cannot say it has been good for me; it has certainly been oddly pleasant. And for this pleasure I must thank my friends, not those of my everyday life, but the unknown numerous friends who have borne with Hornblower during the past twenty-six years since I began writing about him. And that word 'friends' is written in all sincerity, not just as a convenient formula, in the way that a politician might use it on the rostrum, or an actor after the final curtain. It is a remarkable, an extraordinarily pleasant feeling, to know, with comforting certainty (for once) that my work has won for me the friendship – even something like the affection – of people whom I have never met, and never shall meet. I thank them, and it is to them that these words are addressed. There is no need for the formal tag: *Plaudite et valete*.

41

AND so this book is finished; in five minutes I shall be recapping my fountain pen and rising from my chair to stretch. As always it is in the nick of time. A week from today I shall be driving a motor car in the Atlas Mountains, and if an explanation is needed as to why an elderly gentleman not in the best of health should be doing such a thing, I must point out that this is the second day of March and very soon the wildflowers will be blooming in the Atlas Mountains. I shall write one final line; I have always been faintly puzzled about why other writers have ended their books in this way – I have never done so myself until now – but I discover I have a real reason. This book is about writing books, and this is the ultimate item of data.

Berkeley, California. January 12 – March 2, 1963.
Goodbye.

42
POSTSCRIPT, March 5th, 1964

THE date which I wrote on the preceding page has its uses after all; it enables me to know that a year and three days ago I thought I had finished this book, finished everything. During that year there has been some delay over the illustrations, and instead of this book being published (as I expected) in the autumn of 1963 it will be quite surprising if it even appears in the autumn of 1964.

This delay enables me – or compels me – to insert this postscript, which presents an abrupt change of point of view, like most postscripts. With the printer waiting I must write these lines without being quite certain, but to wait until I am certain one way or the other would mean I would not be able to squeeze them into this book. I have an uneasy feeling that history is going to repeat itself. That is one more example of how these things happen. Hornblower is on the move again.

When I finished *Hotspur* Hornblower had reached captain's rank, and it was early in 1805. I chose that date for my own convenience. I did not want to face the complications of involving him in the Trafalgar campaign. And in the next volume – *Atropos* – he suddenly reappears in December 1805 on the Gloucester-London canal, and the lapse of time made it conveniently unnecessary to explain how in the world he got there and what he was doing in the interval. I did not know – I did not even want to know, as I have just said. I wrote those final lines, which appear on the page before this, and went off to the Atlas Mountains (the wildflowers, by the way, were surpassingly lovely) happy in the knowledge that Hornblower was finished, done with, buried.

Now during this past year the ideas have been stirring. It was forged orders that started it. The possibilities of forged orders were exercising my mind – military or naval or air force orders written on the right paper in the correct form and with a convincingly forged signature. I suspected that this basic idea might expand in the usual way, that it might be the parent barnacle of a family of barnacles; it seemed a fair start for a novel in a modern setting. Never in my simplicity during the first happy weeks of liberty did I dwell for a moment on the development which anyone who has read this far in this book probably thought of at once. I completed my visit to Morocco, and went on living my life as inoffensively (in my own opinion) as possible. It was sometime in the autumn of 1963 that the first misgivings assailed me, when the pattern of the barnacles began to assume an ominous shape, or when (to use another

137

and equally hackneyed metaphor) I opened a cupboard door and found a skeleton inside – I saw it plainly despite the speed with which I slammed the door on it.

It was the most singular coincidence, and I declare it to be a coincidence even though I am certain that the psychologists (and psychiatrists) would shake their heads pityingly over my self-deception. There were only seven or eight months, in the latter part of 1805, of Hornblower's life unaccounted for, and I was thinking about forged orders. Yet there it was; forged orders could play a vital part in the campaign of Trafalgar, particularly in the opening moves of that campaign, and here was Hornblower unemployed. There was a certain need to tell what Hornblower was doing during those vital months when Britain's fate was being decided at sea – and here was a job simply ready-made for him, even though I had once thought the job might be done in Scapa Flow in 1916 or 1940 or in the Pentagon in 1953. As far as the Napoleonic Wars were concerned the idea fitted into 1805 and into no other time, and at no other time was Hornblower available to be involved in it, and there was no one more suited to the occasion than Hornblower. Surely the most sceptical psychiatrist, the most cynical reader, will agree that there was a considerable element of coincidence about all this.

It was with actual apprehension, it was with a reluctance never before observed, that last autumn, as I shaved or ran my eye along my library shelves to select a book, I found the barnacle-grown timbers rising to the surface to mock me with a display of new growth. All that growth – which normally would have occasioned vast pleasure – was now a source of bitterness because every new barnacle was another nail pulled out of Hornblower's coffin. In fact he was out of his coffin altogether; his was the skeleton in the cupboard, and while it was there, until he was decently buried again, his ghost refused exorcism. Every added fragment of plot made it the more necessary to include him in it; it was a plot that could only revolve around Hornblower, and could only apply to 1805.

New Year's Day, 1964, found me in Maui and it was there – in a place as far removed from the Trafalgar campaign in space and time and atmosphere as it is possible to conceive – that I had to give up the struggle and abandon the other work which I had undertaken and allow events to take their course.

Since that time they have done so in the usual fashion. The stage has now been reached where it is necessary occasionally to refer to my reference library to check up on facts so as to decide whether some new turn in the plot is technically possible. This morning, before I began today's work (the second

138

day of work on this essay) I found myself turning the pages of encyclopaedias, and taking down Boswell's *Life of Johnson*, in the endeavour to increase, and renew, my small knowledge of the Rev. Dr Dodd who was hanged for forgery in 1777; what Dodd did then has some sort of bearing on what Hornblower might do in 1805 and on what I might do in 1964.

Now, at this very moment of writing, I begin this paragraph having returned to my desk after taking a turn round the room, and the fact that I actually walked instead of just standing up is an indication of the intensity of my present feelings. The future hangs in the balance; another novel is becoming a possibility. Nor is that all. I have to finish this essay today in order to insert it in this book – not only is the printer waiting but the Greek Islands are waiting; I am, when present work and future work leave anything over for sane thinking, making preparations for an immediate departure to the Eastern Mediterranean. The poppies of Greece are intruding themselves upon my mental vision and the siren song that Ulysses heard is stealing on my inward ear. But how much of the one will I really see, and how much of the other will I really hear? This is the period of the deepest abstraction. Fresh links in the chain will be presenting themselves, and (judging by long experience) there will be times when selection has to be made, when one link will have to be, reluctantly, discarded in favour of another, and links that had once appeared tried and true will have to be tested against the standards of real history. What will I care about the Street of the Knights when it is essential that I should know, immediately, how many ships of the line accompanied Nelson to the West Indies?

All this sounds as if I were going to write the novel, but of course that is quite uncertain. Plots have presented themselves before, to be discarded in the end, when the novel finally appears to be not worth writing, or distasteful, or too fragile. That may easily be the case with this one; I would not have written this chapter about it if it were not a matter of now or never.

Supposing I were to write the novel? Supposing (that old doubt – one of the few things that grows stronger with age) I live to complete it? Then somewhere soon after the first week in July, when I am home again, I shall find myself sitting here, where I am sitting now, with this same pen in my hand and this same writing pad in front of me and I shall be writing the figure '1' at the top of the page and launching myself once more on to the toboggan slide, committing myself to the daily hours of visualization and the months of fatigue. Perhaps then – it is an odd thought – I shall look back with envy on the pleasant hours I have spent in this current exercise. Perhaps some time in

October I shall recap my pen and rise stiffly from my desk and come hesitatingly back to life. Until then – perhaps —

The last word I wrote at the end of the last chapter was 'goodbye'. Now I have written it again, with feelings equally strong.